KP

Contents

D1103499

Licence

Text © Carole Creary and Gay Wilson
© 2004 Scholastic Ltd

Published by Scholastic Ltd, Villiers House,
Clarendon Avenue, Leamington Spa,
Warwickshire CV32 5PR

Printed by Bell & Bain Ltd, Glasgow

1234567890   4567890123

British Library Cataloguing-in-Publication Data
A catalogue record for this book is available from
the British Library.

ISBN 0-439-98493-9

**Visit our website at
www.scholastic.co.uk**

CD Developed in association with
Footmark Media Ltd

Authors
Carole Creary and Gay Wilson

Editor
Christine Harvey

Assistant Editors
Roanne Charles
Barbara Newby

Series Designer
Joy Monkhouse

Designer
Catherine Mason

Cover photographs
© Photodisc,
SODA,
Ingram Publishing

Acknowledgements

Extracts from the National Curriculum for England © Crown copyright material is reproduced with the permission of the Controller of HMSO and the Queen's Printer for Scotland.

Every effort has been made to trace copyright holders and the publishers apologise for any omissions.

List of resources on the CD-ROM

The page numbers refer to the teacher's notes provided in this book.

INTRODUCTION

This book and CD-ROM support the teaching and learning set out in the QCA Scheme of Work for science in Year 2. The CD provides a large bank of visual and oral resources. This book provides teacher's notes to accompany the CD resources, which contain background information, ideas for discussion and activities, along with photocopiable pages to support the teaching. All have been specifically chosen to meet the requirements for resources listed in the six QCA units for Year 2. Some additional resources and ideas have also been included to enable teachers to develop and broaden these areas of study if they wish. These include stories, simple information sheets and worksheets to help children clarify their thinking or record things they find out.

The resources and activities are not a structure for teaching in themselves, but are designed to provide a basis for discussion and activities that focus on the knowledge, skills and understanding required by the National Curriculum for science. Some of the ideas build on the National Curriculum requirements and help to broaden the children's experiences.

The children are encouraged, through using the resources on the CD and their accompanying activities, to develop such skills as observing, questioning, describing, sorting, sequencing, finding out, speaking, listening, reading, writing and drawing.

Links with other subjects

Literacy
There are a number of close links between the topics covered in this book and work on literacy. The discussion activities contribute directly to the requirements for speaking and listening. Some of the stories, poems and information sheets could be used in shared reading during the Literacy Hour, or to provide a stimulus for shared, guided or independent writing. There is considerable opportunity for the children to develop their independent writing skills as they produce leaflets or diaries, or write simple poems using the word cards. Pictures from the CD could be printed in order to stimulate children's independent writing or to illustrate it.

Maths
Skills such as counting, matching, ordering or sequencing are essential to both science and maths. Many of the suggested activities in this book require the children to use these skills. For example, creating a tally chart to show paper use (page 53) encourages counting and data collection skills. Measuring skills are fostered when children measure the distance that wheeled toys have travelled during an investigation (page 60). Sorting is an important mathematical and science skill and the activities allow children to have many opportunities to practice it, for example when sorting foods into different groups (page 12).

History
Children can begin to understand how things change and develop over time. For instance, in learning about processes to develop materials children can discover the history of paper (page 58). Talking about the fact that glass was made by the Egyptians as long as 2000 years ago helps children to understand that many materials used today have a long history of usefulness and development.

Art and design
Many of the activities suggested in the teacher's notes encourage children to use art and design to extend their understanding of a particular concept. For example, making an observational drawing of a flower (page 36) encourages close observation and an understanding of line and shape. Collage is used to reinforce children's understanding of the properties of some materials as well as developing their feeling for texture and an aesthetic awareness of colour (page 53).

HOW TO USE THE CD-ROM

Windows NT users

If you use Windows NT you may see the following error message: 'The procedure entry point Process32First could not be located in the dynamic link library KERNEL32.dll'. Click on **OK** and the CD will autorun with no further problems.

Setting up your computer for optimal use

On opening, the CD will alert you if changes are needed in order to operate the CD at its optimal use. There are three changes you may be advised to make:

Viewing resources at their maximum screen size

To see images at their maximum screen size, your screen display needs to be set to 800 x 600 pixels. In order to adjust your screen size you will need to **Quit** the program.

If using a PC, open the **Control Panel**. Select **Display** and then **Settings**. Adjust the **Desktop Area** to 800 x 600 pixels. Click on **OK** and then restart the program.

If using a Mac, from the **Apple** menu select **Control Panels** and then **Monitors** to adjust the screen size.

Adobe Acrobat Reader

To print high-quality versions of images and to view and print the photocopiable pages on the CD you need **Adobe Acrobat Reader** installed on your computer. If you do not have it installed already, a version is provided on the CD. To install this version **Quit** the 'Ready Resources' program.

If using a PC, right-click on the **Start** menu on your desktop and choose **Explore**. Click on the + sign to the left of the CD drive entitled 'Ready Resources' and open the folder called 'Acrobat Reader Installer'. Run the program contained in this folder to install **Adobe Acrobat Reader**.

If using a Mac, double click on the 'Ready Resources' icon on the desktop and on the 'Acrobat Reader Installer' folder. Run the program contained in this folder to install **Adobe Acrobat Reader**.

PLEASE NOTE: If you do not have **Adobe Acrobat Reader** installed, you will not be able to print high-quality versions of images, or to view or print photocopiable pages (although these are provided in the accompanying book and can be photocopied).

QuickTime

In order to view the videos and listen to the audio on this CD you will need to have **QuickTime version 5 or later** installed on your computer. If you do not have it installed already, or have an older version of **QuickTime**, the latest version is provided on the CD. If you choose to install this version, **Quit** the 'Ready Resources' program.

If using a PC, right-click on the **Start** menu on your desktop and choose **Explore**. Click on the + sign to the left of the CD drive that is entitled 'Ready Resources' and open the folder called 'QuickTime Installer'. Run the program contained in this folder to install **QuickTime**.

If using a Mac, double click on the 'Ready Resources' CD icon on the desktop and then on the 'Acrobat Reader Installer' folder. Run the program contained in this folder to install **QuickTime**.

PLEASE NOTE: If you do not have **QuickTime** installed you will be unable to view the films.

Menu screen

▶ Click on the **Resource Gallery** of your choice to view the resources available under that topic.
▶ Click on **Complete Resource Gallery** to view all the resources available on the CD.
▶ Click on **Photocopiable Resources (PDF format)** to view a list of the photocopiables provided in the book that accompanies this CD.
▶ **Back**: click to return to the **opening screen**. Click **Continue** to move to the **Menu screen**.
▶ **Quit**: click **Quit** to close the menu program and progress to the **Quit screen.** If you quit from the **Quit screen** you will exit the CD. If you do not quit you will return to the **Menu screen**.

Resource Galleries

▶ **Help**: click **Help** to find support on accessing and using images.
▶ **Back to menu**: click here to return to the **Menu screen**.
▶ **Quit:** click here to move to the **Quit screen** – see **Quit** above.

Viewing images

Small versions of each image are shown in the Resource Gallery. Click and drag the slider on the slide bar to scroll through the images in the Resource Gallery, or click on the arrows to move the images frame by frame. Roll the pointer over an image to see the caption.

▶ Click on an image to view the screen-sized version of it.
▶ To return to the Resource Gallery click on **Back to Resource Gallery**.

Viewing videos

Click on the video icon of your choice in the Resource Gallery. In order to view the videos on this CD, you will need to have **QuickTime** installed on your computer (see 'Setting up your computer for optimal use' above).

Once at the video screen, use the buttons on the bottom of the video screen to operate the video. The slide bar can be used for a fast forward and rewind. To return to the Resource Gallery click on **Back to Resource Gallery**.

Listening to sound recordings

Click on the required sound icon. Use the buttons or the slide bar to hear the sound. A transcript will be displayed on the viewing screen where appropriate. To return to the Resource Gallery, click on **Back to Resource Gallery**.

Printing

Click on the image to view it (see 'Viewing images' above). There are two print options:

Print using Acrobat enables you to print a high-quality version of an image. Choosing this option means that the image will open as a read-only page in **Adobe Acrobat** and in order to access these files you will need to have already installed **Adobe Acrobat Reader** on your computer (see 'Setting up your computer for optimal use' above). To print the selected resource, select **File** and then **Print**. Once you have printed the resource **minimise** or **close** the Adobe screen using — or **X** in the top right-hand corner of the screen. Return to the Resource Gallery by clicking on **Back to Resource Gallery**.

Simple print enables you to print a lower quality version of the image without the need to use **Adobe Acrobat Reader**. Select the image and click on the **Simple print** option. After printing, click on **Back to Resource Gallery**.

Slideshow presentation

If you would like to present a number of resources without having to return to the Resource Gallery and select a new image each time, you can compile a slideshow. Click on the **+** tabs at the top of each image in the Resource Gallery you would like to include in your presentation (pictures, sound and video can be included). It is important that you click on the images in the order in which you would like to view them (a number will appear on each tab to confirm the order). If you would like to change the order, click on **Clear slideshow** and begin again. Once you have selected your images – up to a maximum of 20 – click on **Play slideshow** and you will be presented with the first of your selected resources. To move to the next selection in your slideshow click on **Next slide**, to see a previous resource click on **Previous slide**. You can end your slideshow presentation at any time by clicking on **Resource Gallery**. Your slideshow selection will remain selected until you **Clear slideshow** or return to the **Menu screen**.

Viewing on an interactive whiteboard or data projector

Resources can be viewed directly from the CD. To make viewing easier for a whole class, use a large monitor, data projector or interactive whiteboard. For group, paired or individual work, the resources can be viewed from the computer screen.

Photocopiable resources (PDF format)

To view or print a photocopiable resource page, click on the required title in the list and the page will open as a read-only page in **Adobe Acrobat**. In order to access these files you will need to have already installed **Adobe Acrobat Reader** on your computer (see 'Setting up your computer for optimal use' above). To print the selected resource select **File** and then **Print**. Once you have printed the resource **minimise** or **close** the Adobe screen using — or **X** in the top right-hand corner of the screen. This will take you back to the list of PDF files. To return to the **Menu screen**, click on **Back**.

HEALTH AND GROWTH

Content and skills

This chapter links to Unit 2A 'Health and growth' of the QCA Scheme of Work for science at Key Stage 1. The Health and Growth Resource Gallery on the CD-ROM, together with the teacher's notes and photocopiable pages in this chapter, can be used when teaching this unit.

As with the QCA Scheme of Work, this chapter looks at how animals, including humans, grow and reproduce. Children can use ideas about feeding and growth learned in this unit to help them understand some of the ways in which we need to look after ourselves in order to stay healthy.

The accompanying teacher's notes in the book contain background information about the photographs on the CD-ROM and include ways of using the resources as a whole class, for group work or as individuals. Some of the activities suggested will link with other areas of the curriculum, such as English, maths or art. Wherever possible, the activities encourage the children to ask questions and develop an enquiring approach to their learning.

Resources on the CD-ROM

The CD-ROM contains photographs that lead to discussion and work on health, such as visits to the doctor and dentist. Photographs detailing the range and variety of food that we need to eat for health and growth, pictures of babies, toddlers and animals and their young are also included.

Photocopiable pages

The photocopiable pages in the book are also provided in PDF format on the CD-ROM and can be printed out from there. They include:
► word cards containing the essential vocabulary for the topic
► a story
► a rhyme
► writing frames.

Science skills

Skills such as observing, questioning, finding out, describing, sorting, sequencing, listening, speaking, reading, writing and drawing are involved in the activities provided in the teacher's notes. Putting foods into particular food groups will help children's sorting and matching skills, as will sorting medicines from sweets. Asking questions and listening to the ideas of others will help to develop questioning, speaking and listening skills.

Photographs © Ingram Publishing

NOTES ON THE CD-ROM RESOURCES

KEEPING HEALTHY

An injection

Most children will have been to the doctor for an injection and may not remember it as a very pleasant experience. This picture can be used to talk about the benefits of injections in terms of keeping us healthy by preventing diseases, as well as helping to make us better when we are ill. It can also be used as the basis for a sensitive discussion about the inappropriate use of injections and to warn the children about this without frightening them. Any such discussion should be within the framework of relevant school policies on the subject.

Discussing the photograph
▶ Talk to the children about what they can see in the photograph and ask if any of them can remember going to the doctor for an injection or whether they have been given an injection in school by a visiting nurse or doctor. What was it like?
▶ Can anyone tell you why they go to the doctor's for injections?
▶ Discuss the benefits of childhood vaccinations and the fact that these prevent some of the diseases that could make them ill, especially when they are children. Explain that one prick with a needle may stop them from being poorly in the future.
▶ Talk about the inappropriate use of syringes and needles and tell the children that they must never touch or pick up such things if they find them outside.
▶ Discuss such conditions as diabetes where some children might have to have an injection quite often, sometimes several times a day, in order to keep them well, and that in this case their mummy or daddy might give the injections or they may do it for themselves. Make sure that the children understand that medicines can be beneficial and that we take them when we are ill to help us to get better or to prevent us from becoming ill, but that they can also be very dangerous if we take them when we don't need them.
▶ Remind the children that they should never take any medicine that they find and should only ever take medicines that are given to them by a responsible adult that they know well. Discuss why medicines should always be kept in their original containers and not transferred to such things as pop bottles. Ask the children why they think that medicines are often packed in bottles with safety tops.

Activities
▶ Use the word cards on photocopiable page 15 to help the children understand the main vocabulary when discussing the photograph, such as *injection*, *safety*.
▶ Put a selection of plastic syringes into the water tray and allow the children to play with them. (This will reassure them that not all uses of syringes are bad or dangerous.)
▶ Turn the home corner into a hospital and encourage role play, such as a doctor examining a patient or a nurse giving injections.
▶ Teach the children the rhyme 'Miss Polly' (photocopiable page 17).
▶ Make a collection of packaging of both drugs and sweets (ensuring that all medicine packaging is empty before being brought into the classroom) and ask the children to sort them into two groups. Try to include some medicines that look like sweets, such as cough 'sweets', that the children may put into the sweets group. Use this to reinforce the dangers of eating anything they find that might look like sweets. Read some of the warnings on the drugs packages to the children to reinforce the idea that medicines (drugs) should only be taken when given to them by a parent, carer, doctor or nurse.
▶ Invite a nurse or other health professional into the classroom to talk about what visits to the doctor or nurse might be like and to remind the children when they will be given medicines safely and why. Ask the children to think about the questions that they might like to ask before the visitor arrives and make a list of these.

The dentist

This picture gives you the opportunity to talk to the children about dental health care in general and going to the dentist in particular. Some children may have experience of going to the dentist and will be able to talk about it, while others will not. Although children need to know about caring for their teeth, it is a subject that still has to be tackled with sensitivity. There is the possibility that there will be children in the class who don't clean their teeth on a regular basis or who do not own their own toothbrush.

Discussing the photograph

▶ Talk to the children about what they can see in the photograph. If any of them have ever been to the dentist ask them to tell the others about it. (Going to the dentist these days is normally a pleasant experience for children, but it is wise to nip any horror stories in the bud!)

▶ Discuss how to care for teeth, including such things as regular brushing, in particular brushing last thing before going to bed and not eating too many sweet things.

▶ Have any of the children started to lose their first (or milk) teeth?

▶ Talk about how we lose our first set of teeth when we are about six or seven years old and grow a new set of adult teeth. Explain that these teeth will have to last for the rest of our lives and so it is important that we take care of them.

Activities

▶ Role play the correct way to brush teeth with the children.

▶ Ask the children to look carefully at their teeth in a mirror. Ask them to draw a self-portrait with their mouth open and their teeth showing.

▶ Ask a dental nurse to visit the classroom and talk to the children about caring for their teeth.

▶ Read the poem 'Oh I Wish I'd Looked After me Teeth!' by Pam Ayers in *The Works* to the children and discuss its meaning with them.

FOOD

Vegetables, Fruit, Bread, Rice, Cheese, Meat, Fish, Cake and biscuits

These photographs show foods that fall into the four main food groups that the children should be aware of at this stage These are fruit and vegetables; cereals; meat, fish, eggs and dairy; and high-energy foods. Children often think that some foods are bad for them – sweets, for example and don't realise that nothing is intrinsically bad as long as we eat a balanced diet and don't eat too much of any one thing, particularly foods that are high in sugars and fats. Vegetables shown include carrots, onions, cauliflower, cabbage, peas and peppers. Fruit shown includes apples, bananas, grapes, melon, strawberries, peaches, lemons, limes and kiwi fruit. The bread shown includes a variety of types and shapes of loaves and rolls, some with seeds on them. The rice shown includes both white and brown rice. The cheeses are all hard cheeses and include Edam and Emmental. The meat shown is red meat, including steak and minced beef. The fish counter shows a variety of fish. Some are whole while others have been filleted ready for cooking. The cake and biscuits are also shown with ice cream and crisps, all high in sugar and fat.

Discussing the photographs

▶ Look at all the photographs in turn and ask the children if they can tell what type of food is depicted in each one.

▶ Ask the children if they eat foods from each of these groups.

▶ Discuss the fact that some people are vegetarians and do not eat meat or fish, and that some people don't eat anything at all that comes from an animal. Talk about the fact that this can be because of their religion or because they don't like the idea of killing animals for food. Sometimes it is because people don't like the taste or feel of, for example, meat.

▶ Ask the children if they know why we need food and water? Ask, *What would happen if we had no food or water?* Talk about the fact that an adequate, balanced diet is necessary for us to grow and stay healthy.

▶ Talk about the fact that no food is bad for us except if we eat too much of it and too much of one type of food.

▶ Look together at the pictures again, one by one, and ask if the children can identify some of the different things in them. For example, can they name some of the fruit and vegetables, cheeses and meat.

▶ Talk about the four different food groups that the pictures show and what they give our bodies. For example, fruit and vegetables keep us healthy; meat, fish, eggs and dairy products help us grow; cereals and high-energy foods give us energy.

Activities

▶ Ask the children to write down what some of the foods in each of the photographs taste like. Use the word cards on photocopiable page 16 to help them. For instance, they could write *Grapes taste sweet*, *Crisps taste salty*. Then ask them to number the foods they chose in order of taste preference.

▶ Ask the children to look at the photographs and to write down the names of some of the foods that come in each of the four groups. Use the 'Food groups' photocopiable sheet (page 20) to direct the task. Ask them to add at least one food to each list that is not shown in the photographs.

▶ Use cooking sessions over a four-week period to make a dish using ingredients mainly from each food group in turn. For example, cheese on toast, a vegetable salad or fruit salad, bread or rolls, cake.

▶ Ask the children to paint a poster about healthy eating. They could use the word cards on photocopiable page 14 to support any writing they want to put on it, words such as *variety*, *balanced*.

▶ Collect empty boxes, such as shoe, chocolate or biscuit boxes, and ask the children to decorate them to look like lunch boxes. Then ask them to fill them with a model of a balanced packed lunch made out of reclaimed materials or dried and painted clay.

▶ Ask groups of children to identify simple favourite dishes. You could make a class list of these, or a cookery book.

▶ Read the story 'Cooking lunch' (photocopiable page 18) to the children. Use it as a starting point to talk about why a balanced diet is important.

ANIMALS AND THEIR YOUNG

Human, Human baby, Adult rat, Baby rats, Adult blue tit, Blue-tit nestlings, Ladybird, Ladybird larvae, Adult kangaroo, Joey

These separate images of adults and their babies include some that may be less familiar to children, such as the ladybird and ladybird larvae and the kangaroo and joey. (If Ready Resources: Science 1 is available, these photographs can be used in conjunction with the more familiar animals and their young supplied in the 'Living things' section ('Animals and their young') to revisit and reinforce the earlier learning.) Children need to know that all animals produce young that then grow into adults. If it fits in with your school policy and it is considered appropriate, the term *reproduce* could be introduced at this stage.

Discussing the photographs

▶ Create a slideshow using all the photographs to show to the children. Find out if they know that all the creatures in the photographs are animals, including the humans.

▶ Discuss some of the things that are common to all animals. For example, they all need food and water and they all have babies (reproduce).

▶ Make slideshows of the photographs of each pair of adult and young and ensure that the children understand that the babies grow into adults that resemble their parents. Talk about the fact that some newly born babies already look very like their parents and that some are very different. For example, a human baby looks recognisably human, while a ladybird larva looks nothing like an adult ladybird.

Activities

▶ Using copies of the photographs, ask the children if they know the names of all the adult animals. Get them to label the photographs to support their learning and to use as part of a class display. The word cards on photocopiable page 13 could be added, using words such as *have young*, *reproduce*.

▶ Ask the children to match the photographs of the adults to their babies and to explain why they have put the pairs together. How did they know?

▶ Use copies of the photographs to play snap. The children have to 'snap' the correct adults and babies together.

▶ Let the children play matching pairs. Mount the photographs on card and laminate them for durability. Lay the cards face down on the table and let the children take turns to turn over two cards. If they have an adult and the correct baby they can keep the pair, otherwise the cards are laid face down again for the next child's turn. The child with the most pairs when all the cards have been collected is the winner.

▶ Borrow a pet with their young for a day. Let the children observe and draw the animals, encouraging them to talk about their observations.

BABIES

Baby being fed, Baby being bathed, Baby being changed

Some children may have the experience of having a baby brother or sister and be familiar with the routines of feeding and bathing. These photographs help to illustrate the care and help that a baby requires.

Discussing the photographs

▶ Show the children the photographs and discuss what each shows.

▶ Talk to the children about the differences between what they can do now and what they were able to do when they were babies.

▶ Ask how they have changed as they have grown. For example, they can now feed themselves, walk and run rather than having to be carried. They can take themselves to the toilet rather than having to wear a nappy, and so on.

▶ Discuss not just the physical changes that have taken place, but also that they can/are beginning to read, to do maths and can generally understand more.

▶ Talk about any younger brothers and sisters the children may have at home and get the children to tell you about things that they can do that their younger siblings cannot. Ask the children to tell the class about some of the things that they do at home to help with their younger brothers and sisters.

▶ Discuss with the children what their older siblings or cousins can now do for themselves but that they, themselves, still need help with.

Activities

▶ Look at the photographs again. Ask the children to think about the differences between babies and toddlers and their capabilities. Make a class list.

▶ Ask the children to draw or paint pictures of some of the things babies need help with, such as dressing, feeding and bathing.

▶ Invite a parent with a young baby into the classroom for the children to see. Ask the parent to talk about some of the things that the baby has to have done for it. If possible, ask the parent to change, feed and bath the baby while the children watch.

▶ Use the photocopiable 'Can do, can't do!' (photocopiable page 21) for the children to match things that they can do and things that a baby can do.

NOTES ON THE PHOTOCOPIABLE PAGES

Word cards   PAGE 13

These word cards contain some of the basic vocabulary for the children to use and learn when learning about 'Health and growth'. They include:
▶ words relating to life processes
▶ words relating to health – both healthy eating and medicinal safety
▶ words relating to taste.
Read through the word cards with the children. Ask which words the children have heard before. Are there any words they don't understand?

Activities

▶ Spread the word cards on a table and ask the children to find specific words.

▶ Ask the children to sort out all the words that are concerned with health.

▶ Can they sort out the words concerned with growing, or those about food?

Miss Polly

PAGE 17

This is a copy of the traditional rhyme 'Miss Polly' for the children to learn and say. It also lends itself very well to actions when being recited.

Discussing the rhyme

▶ Sing or say the rhyme to the children. Talk about why Miss Polly needed to call the doctor. Have the children ever had the doctor come to see them at home?

▶ Discuss what happens when we are ill. What might we take to help make us better? Where would we get medicines?

▶ Remind the children that they should never take any pills or medicines they find, as these could be dangerous.

Activities

▶ Give the children a copy each of the rhyme and let them learn it. Then say it together and make up some actions to go with it.

▶ Turn the home corner into a hospital or Doctor's surgery and encourage role play.

▶ Ask the children to paint pictures to illustrate the rhyme and add these to a large copy of the rhyme to form a class display. Use the word cards on photocopiable pages 14 and 15, such as *healthy*, *medicines*, to add to the display.

▶ Show the children how to use a forehead thermometer and how it shows body temperature by changing colour.

Cooking lunch

PAGE 18

This story about cooking lunch for a group of elderly people focuses on ensuring that the lunches that are made are balanced across the main food groups.

Discussing the story

▶ Read the story to the children and discuss what is meant by a balanced diet.

▶ Talk about the fact that humans of all ages need to eat a balanced diet to keep healthy, not just children who are growing and changing.

▶ Why do the children think that Mum asked the pensioners about their favourite foods? (Older people sometimes have a poor appetite, but may be persuaded to eat a favourite dish. Eating a favourite dish will also add to their enjoyment.)

▶ Ask them how Mum ensured that the pensioners had a balanced meal each week when she cooked for them.

Activities

▶ Ask some children for their favourite main courses and others for their favourite puddings. Make a list of these and then try and put them together to make a balanced meal as a class. Discuss why things such as a meat pie and treacle pudding should not be put together as a meal.

▶ Turn the home corner into a café. Let the children devise menus and make models of meals from reclaimed materials or salt dough.

Food groups

PAGE 20

Children can use this page to show their knowledge of different food groups. Remind the children of what they have learned about food groups before they complete this sheet and ask them to tell you some foods that go into each group before they start. Can they remember what the foods in each group contribute to a balanced diet?

Can do, can't do!

PAGE 21

This is a sheet for the children to draw a picture of themselves and a baby and to match things that they can and can't do unaided to the pictures. Remind the children of what they have learned about how humans change as they grow and of the things they can and can't do at various stages, if necessary. Read through the sheet with the children and make sure they understand what they have to do.

Life processes word cards

grow

growth

move

have young

reproduce

feed

Health word cards (1)

diet

variety

balanced

exercise

healthy

unhealthy

Health word cards (2)

germ

medicines

safety

packaging

injection

Taste word cards

salty

sweet

sour

bitter

spicy

Miss Polly

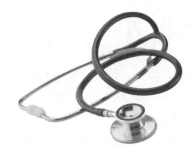

Miss Polly had a dolly
Who was sick, sick, sick,
So she called for the doctor
To be quick, quick, quick.
The doctor came
With his bag and his hat,
And he knocked on the door
With a rat-a-tat-tat.

He looked at the dolly
And he shook his head,
And he said, "Miss Polly,
Put her straight to bed."
He wrote out a paper
For a pill, pill, pill.
"I'll be back in the morning
With the bill, bill, bill."

Cooking lunch

"Mum, Mum, get up. Remember what we're doing today."

Jaz and Toby bounced on the bed to wake their mother. She opened her eyes and groaned as she looked at the clock.

"Do you two know what time it is?" she asked. "It's far too early. Off you go and play for a while."

The twins were very excited. Not only was it the first week of the holidays, but Mum had promised that they could go with her and help cook the meal for the local pensioners' lunch club. They both loved cooking. From when they were very young they had stood on small stools beside their mum in the kitchen to help her. Jaz liked cooking puddings best and Toby liked making savouries. They went off quietly to play for a bit while Mum got ready.

After breakfast they set off. It was still quite early, but Mum said it would take a while to get the lunch ready and it was her first time so she wanted to be there early to make sure everything was OK.

The twins knew what Mum was going to cook for lunch: cottage pie with carrots, peas and gravy, and after that apple crumble and custard.

"How do we know that they'll like it?" asked Toby, skipping beside Mum.

"Well," said Mum, "I asked the other lady who cooked the lunch before I said I'd do it and she said that most of them like it."

"Didn't she ask them what they like to eat?" asked Jaz.

"I don't think she did, Jaz," Mum said thoughtfully. "She gave them what she thought they would like and if there wasn't too much left on their plates at the end she knew it was alright."

"I think we should ask them," said Jaz, remembering how much she hated some things, like cabbage and rhubarb.

"That's a very good idea, Jaz," said Mum. "We will ask them."

When they got to the hall, before they began, Mum asked the man who ran the office for enough paper for all the pensioners to have a piece each.

"What's that for?" asked Toby.

"What I'm going to do," said Mum, "is ask each person to write down their favourite lunch – a main course and a pudding – on their piece of paper and then we'll cook each one in turn, so that everyone gets their favourite lunch within a few weeks. Then, when we've cooked all the lunches, we'll ask them whether they want us to begin at the beginning again or whether they want us to change anything."

The twins thought this was a great idea.

Photograph © Nova Developments

◼ SCHOLASTIC
PHOTOCOPIABLE

Soon they were very busy helping to lay the tables and wash the carrots and potatoes. They got enough plates out for Mum to put in the plate warmer and enough dishes to put the apple crumble in when it was time for pudding. There were eight pensioners coming for lunch.

The lunch looked and smelled very good to the twins and most people seemed to enjoy it, though there were one or two plates with quite a lot left on them and one lady did not want pudding at all. The pensioners seemed to get on really well together and there was a lot of talking and laughing. There were five ladies and three men. One of the ladies was Indian and was dressed in a beautiful sari. Jaz thought it was a lovely colour. One of the men was from Hong Kong, Mum said, but he dressed like everyone else. There was also a lovely lady who came originally from the Caribbean but had lived in England nearly all her life. Her grandchildren were about Jaz and Toby's age, she told them.

When everyone was having their coffee Mum gave out the pieces of paper and asked them to make a note of their favourite lunch so that she could cook what they wanted especially for them. They were very surprised and pleased because no one had ever asked them what they wanted before.

They all wrote on their papers, then Mum read them out. What a surprise! The pensioners said that some of the things had never been cooked for them at the lunch club. Food like banana fritters, fruit salad with mangoes and guavas in; okra and sweet potatoes instead of the usual vegetables; chicken in black bean sauce with bean sprouts; fish and chips; steak and kidney pie; and ham and eggs. There were requests for chicken salad and rice pudding, Bakewell tart and pineapple and ice cream.

"Well," said Mum, "everyone likes something different!" The pensioners laughed and all said they would like to try everything and change the list when they had. So that was agreed, but Mum said that she would cook all the things on the main dish list and all the things on the pudding list, but not always the favourite main dish and pudding on the

same day. In that way she could 'mix and match' the meals so that people were getting a properly balanced meal every week with all the food groups they needed in it.

Everyone thought that that was a really good idea. So did the twins, because they had been learning about food groups and how to eat a good balanced diet at school.

Food groups

▷ Write the names of some foods that go in each food group. Draw pictures of them.

Fruit and vegetables

Names _____

_____

Meat, fish, eggs and dairy products

Names _____

_____

Cereals

Names _____

_____

High-energy foods

Names _____

_____

Can do, can't do!

▷ Draw a picture of yourself in the top box and a picture of a baby in the bottom box.

This is me.

▷ Draw lines from the picture to the things you can do for yourself.

Dress	**Feed**	**Go to school**	**Go to bed**
	Go to the toilet	**Sit up**	**Read a book**
Write	**Have a bath**	**Clean my teeth**	**Walk**

This is a baby.

▷ Draw lines to the things that a baby needs help to do.

PLANTS AND ANIMALS IN THE LOCAL ENVIRONMENT

Content and skills

This chapter links to Unit 2B 'Plants and animals in the local environment' of the QCA Scheme of Work for science at Key Stage 1. The Plants and Animals in the Local Environment Resource Gallery on the CD-ROM, together with the teacher's notes and photocopiable pages in this chapter, can be used when teaching this unit.

As with the QCA Scheme of Work, the resources on the CD can help children to learn about plants and animals in their immediate environment and help them to understand that animals and plants reproduce themselves. It is also important that children learn to respect all living things and to handle them with care and consideration. They should also begin to appreciate that the environment can easily be damaged and that they have a part to play in maintaining it so that it provides places where even the smallest plants and animals can live.

The teacher's notes include ways of using the resources on the CD as a whole class, for group work or with individual children. Some of the activities suggested will link with other areas of the curriculum, such as English, maths or art. Wherever possible, the activities encourage the children to ask questions and develop an enquiring approach to their learning.

Resources on the CD-ROM

There are photographs of plants showing flowers and then the same plants when their fruits have developed. Close up photographs show how fruits from different plants vary in size and shape.

There are photographs of animals, such as birds or frogs, with their eggs or very young offspring. There is also a video of a butterfly emerging from a chrysalis.

Photocopiable pages

The photocopiable pages in the book are also provided in PDF format on the CD-ROM and can be printed out from there. They include:
▶ word cards containing the essential vocabulary of the topic
▶ a writing frame.

Science skills

Skills such as observing, questioning, finding out, describing, sorting, sequencing, listening, speaking, reading, writing and drawing are involved in the activities suggested in the teacher's notes. For example, looking closely at fruits and finding the seeds will help children develop observation skills, while filling in the 'Seed watch' writing frame will help them observe and describe the changes that take place as the seed grows into a plant. Asking questions about why creatures are found in particular places and listening to the ideas of others will help to develop questioning, speaking and listening skills.

Photograph © Ingram Publishing

NOTES ON THE CD-ROM RESOURCES

FRUITS AND FLOWERS

> **Dandelions in bloom, Dandelion seed heads, Apple orchard in blossom, Apple trees with fruit, Horse chestnut tree in flower, Horse chestnut fruit**

In Year 1 children learned about growing plants. In this unit they learn more about why plants develop fruits and seeds. The photographs show examples of the wide variety of flowers and fruits that abound. All the examples shown rely on insects, such as bees or hover flies, to pollinate them. Other plants may be pollinated by the wind or by insects, such as moths or beetles or even bats, but the children do not need to learn this at this stage.

The dandelion is a complex flower, consisting of many tiny florets that can each produce a small hard seed. Each of these has its own 'parachute' that enables it to be blown and dispersed by the wind. The apple tree produces many flowers (blossom) which, when fertilised, develop into fleshy fruits that are attractive to animals. They may eat the fruit and discard the seeds at some distance from the parent tree where it may fall to the ground, germinate and grow into another tree.

Horse chestnut trees produce spikes of flowers, sometimes called 'candles'. The fruit of this tree is a hard nut encased in an outer green case that splits to reveal the shiny, brown nut inside.

The terms pollination and fertilisation are often used interchangeably. While children will learn more about this later in their education, it is important that misconceptions are not reinforced. Pollination is the transfer of pollen from one flower to another by various means. Fertilisation is when a male gamete, a pollen grain, fuses with a female gamete, or ova, in the ovary of the plant.

Children need to understand that a plant will not develop fruits if it does not flower, or if the flowers are picked or damaged in some way. If there are no flowers, then there will be no fruit and, therefore, no seeds from which new plants may grow. Many of the plants found around the school may be classified as 'weeds' by the children. Stress that even though we may call them weeds or wild flowers, they are still living things and need to be handled with care.

Discussing the photographs

▶ Ask the children if they know how we get new plants. Explain how new plants grow from seeds.

▶ Look at the photographs of the flowering plants – 'Dandelions in bloom', 'Apple orchard in blossom' and 'Horse chestnut tree in flower'. Ask the children if they can name any of the plants. Have they seen any of them near home or school? Remind the children that trees are also flowering plants.

▶ Look at the photographs of the plants showing fruit – 'Dandelion seed heads', 'Apple trees with fruit', 'Horse chestnut fruit' and discuss these with the children.

▶ Compile a slideshow of the photographs and ask the children about the different parts of the plants that they can see, such as stem or trunk, leaves and flowers. Look particularly at the flowers. Ask, *Are they all the same? How are they different?* For example, are all the flowers the same colour or shape? How are they arranged on the stem? Explain that the dandelion is really lots of tiny flowers grouped together and that each tiny flower can produce a seed. Talk about how the flowers help the plant to produce fruits by attracting pollinating insects, such as bees.

▶ Tell the children how a plant is pollinated, that once the seeds are fertilised they can develop. Discuss how the fruits contain seeds and that the seeds will grow into new plants (see background information above).

▶ Use this opportunity to talk about the need to protect wild flowers. Explain how picking them means that they cannot produce the seeds that would grow into new plants. Encourage the children to adopt a mainly 'Look, but don't pick' attitude, although explain that collecting one example for identification purposes is allowed.

▶ Remind the children that they should never eat any fruit or seeds they find. Many hedgerow fruits look very attractive and tempting, but can in fact be extremely poisonous. The Association for Science Education (ASE) publishes a booklet 'Be Safe' which lists poisonous plants likely to be found in the local environment.

Activities
▶ Ask the children to match the pairs of photographs – plant in flower to the plant bearing fruit. They could use the 'Plant word cards' (photocopiable page 31) to label the photographs.
▶ Take the children out and look for plants around the school. Encourage the children to look up as well as down, to look where they are walking and to tread carefully. Remind them to treat all plants with respect. Tell them to observe the sorts of places where they find any plants. Was the place dry, damp, in shade or in full sun? Remind the children that they should not pick the flowers, but draw them where they are or take photographs.
▶ When out with the children, look for fruits beginning to develop at the base of dying flowers. Roses, wild or cultivated, are very good for this, where you can see the fruit swelling at the base of the flower as it dies off.
▶ Back in the classroom, let the children use simple reference books to find the names of the plants they have found.
▶ Ask the children to make detailed observational drawings of a single flower or leaf that you have brought in. Asking them to concentrate on a particular section of a plant helps them to draw in more detail than asking them to draw a whole plant would. They could use hand lenses to see even more detail.

ANIMAL BEGINNINGS

Frog, Frogspawn, Young bird, Bird's nest with eggs, Snail, Snail eggs

Before teaching this section it is a good idea to place some old flower pots, logs or large stones in corners around the school building or field two or three weeks beforehand. This will ensure that there are places for the children to explore. Remind the children about handling any creatures they find with care and about washing their hands afterwards.

In this unit children are looking at animals found in their immediate environment, which are likely to be things such as snails, worms, caterpillars or perhaps birds feeding from a bird table or feeder in the playground. You may be able to keep a small amount of frogspawn in the classroom if you are doing this unit in the spring. Remember, you may take spawn from a private pond, but that it is illegal to take frogspawn from the wild, to buy it or sell it. Try and return the tadpoles or froglets to the pond they came from.

Discussing the photographs
▶ Remind the children about animals and their babies, and how the babies grow into adults and possibly have babies themselves.
▶ Talk about how even very small animals have babies that grow into adults, but sometimes the babies may look very different from the adults.
▶ Look at the photographs and explain how these animals – frog, snail and bird – lay eggs rather than having live babies, and how the baby animals grow and develop inside the egg outside the animal's body until they are ready to hatch. Ask the children if they can name any other animals that lay eggs.
▶ Talk about how the bird's eggs are different from those of the frog or the snail. The bird's eggs have a hard, opaque shell that varies in colour according to the type of bird. Frog eggs (spawn) are covered in a jelly like substance and the developing tadpole can easily be seen as it grows. Snail eggs are tiny and their shells are almost transparent. The developing baby snails can sometimes be seen inside.
▶ Explain that the baby bird has to use its beak to break out of the hard shell, while the baby snails and tadpoles gradually absorb the jelly as they grow.
▶ Discuss the fact that birds usually build a nest in which to lay their eggs, but frogs have to lay their eggs in water, usually in ponds that are quiet and still. Snails lay their eggs in the earth or under stones.

Activities
▶ Use the word cards on photocopiable page 28 to familiarise the children with key vocabulary, such as *eggs*, *reproduce*, *produce young*.

▶ Show the children a hen's egg. Talk about the shell being strong enough to protect the baby, but thin enough for the baby chick to break when it is ready to hatch. Break the egg onto a plate and talk about how the yolk provides the food for a baby chick to grow. You may wish to stress that not all eggs develop into chicks, as some have not been fertilised. Do not allow the children to touch or taste the raw egg since there is a possible risk of salmonella poisoning.

▶ Take the children out around the school to look for small animals. Encourage them to look under stones and in cracks in walls or fences. Help them identify any creatures found. Small creatures can be taken back to the classroom for identification purposes, but make sure that they are only kept for a very short time and that they are put back where they were found. Show the children how any collecting boxes should be carefully washed out at the end of the session to make sure they are ready for next time and to make sure there are no small creatures lurking in the corners.

▶ Take some frogspawn into the classroom. Let the children observe it using a hand lens to see the eyes and mouths. Find out from simple reference books what tadpoles eat and ask the children to keep a picture diary of their development.

▶ Read the poem 'A black dot' by Libby Houston in *The New Oxford Treasury of Children's Poems*, edited by Michael Harrison and Christopher Stuart-Clark to the children.

▶ Think of as many words as you can that describe the way tadpoles move and behave. Use these words to write tadpole poems.

FRUITS

Tomato, Pepper, Sunflower, Apple, Blackberry, Horse chestnut

Scientifically, the term *fruit* relates to the ripened ovary of a flowering plant that develops to protect the seed or seeds. While children may know that apples and oranges are fruits, they may not understand that tomatoes, peppers, sunflower seeds and horse chestnuts are also fruits of specific plants as, indeed, are peas and cucumbers.

Many fruits are also a form of advertising by plants in order to get their seeds dispersed so that new plants can be propagated. They are often brightly coloured to attract animals, including humans, to eat them and spread the seed either by discarding the seeds or by dispersing them in their droppings. However, children should learn that not all brightly coloured fruits are good to eat and that they should never eat any fruits or berries they find unless a responsible adult tells them that it is safe to do so.

Discussing the photographs

▶ Show the children the photographs and ask if they recognise any of the items in them. Can they name any? Have they eaten any of them before? Which of them do they think are fruits?

▶ Explain to the children that all the photographs are of fruits and that fruits are formed by plants to protect their seeds or to help to get the seeds scattered so that new plants can grow.

▶ Point out the seeds in each of the photographs. Explain that the middle of the sunflower is made up of ripening seeds. Discuss where the seeds are to be found in the blackberries. Which part of the horse chestnut is the seed? Explain how the outer case splits and that the shiny, brown nut inside is really the fruit or one big seed that, given the right conditions, could grow into a new horse chestnut tree.

▶ Tell the children that plants often have highly coloured and attractive fruits so that animals, including humans, will eat them and help to spread the seeds about.

▶ Stress the dangers of eating any unknown fruits the children find. Explain that animals can often safely eat fruits that are poisonous to humans.

▶ Ask if any of the children know why plants produce seeds. Ask what needs to happen to a seed to turn it into a new plant. Discuss how it needs warmth and moisture in order to germinate.

Photograph © Ingram Publishing

Activities

▶ Make a collection of real fruits for the children to handle and match to the photographs. Ask questions, such as *What do they feel like? How do they smell?* Look carefully at the fruits and cut them open so the children can find the seeds. Add single-stone fruits, such as mango, peach or avocado. Ask, *How are the seeds in these fruits different?*

▶ Take the children out and look for other seeds in fruits or seed heads from hedgerows or flower beds, such as rose hips, wallflowers, honesty, and so on. Make sure that the children wash their hands after handling fruits and seeds and remind them about not putting any seeds in their mouths.

▶ Find a flower with an obvious ovary swelling at the base, such as a rose. Explain to the children that as the flower dies the fruit swells and the seeds form. Cut the ovary open to show the children the developing seeds. It is interesting if you can find several at different stages of development for them to observe.

▶ Let the children plant some of the seeds found in either fruits or seed heads. Some seeds make take quite a long time to germinate. For example, acorns and conkers will take months before the seedlings appear, while others, such as poppies or oil seed rape, germinate quite quickly. The children could use the 'Seed watch' sheet (photocopiable page 34) to record the progress of the seeds. If children have planted different seeds, they could compare the time they took to germinate and their rate of growth.

▶ Share a melon out between the children. Save, wash and dry the seeds. As a class, find out, by sticking the seeds on to strips of paper, how many number lines of ten can be made with the seeds from one melon. Ask, *How many seeds were in the melon altogether?* Ask the children if they think a new melon plant could be grown from each seed?

ANIMAL CHANGES

Video: Butterfly emerging from chrysalis

This video clip shows a butterfly emerging from its pupa or chrysalis. Adult butterflies usually mate in the spring, after which the female lays her eggs, often on a particular sort of plant, depending on the type of butterfly. Tiny caterpillars emerge from the eggs after about two weeks and, after eating their egg shells, they start eating the leaves of the plant they are on.

The caterpillar's skin is quite hard and cannot stretch, so, as the caterpillar grows, the skin gets tighter and eventually splits. The caterpillar sheds this old skin and underneath it has a new, soft skin. The caterpillar swells up to its new size before the skin dries and becomes stiff. A caterpillar may do this several times before it is big enough to change into a butterfly. When it is big enough, the caterpillar finds a safe place and sheds its skin or moults for the last time. This time there is a different sort of skin underneath. This is harder and will protect the caterpillar while it changes into a butterfly. Inside the pupa or chrysalis profound changes take place where the caterpillar breaks down and is reformed in the shape of a butterfly. This usually takes about two weeks, although some species may stay in this state over the winter.

Children in Year 2 at will need to understand that not all animals have the same life cycles, including many animals in their own environment.

Discussing the video

▶ Show the children the video. Ask them what the animal at the end of the clip is.

▶ Talk about how a butterfly lays its eggs and how they hatch into tiny caterpillars. Explain how a caterpillar grows and grows until it is ready to change into a chrysalis and then into a butterfly.

▶ Talk about how the butterfly has emerged from the chrysalis or pupa, and how it needs to rest and stretch its wings and allow them to dry before it can fly off.

▶ Talk about how the animal has changed on its way to becoming an adult. Discuss whether or not you can tell from looking at a caterpillar or chrysalis what sort of adult animal it will change into.

▶ Ask the children if they think all animals go through these sorts of changes. Can they think of any other animals that go through several changes before they become an adult, for example a frog, dragonfly, mayfly, and so on.

Activities
▶ Use words such as *caterpillar* and *chrysalis* on the word cards on photocopiable page 28 when discussing the video.
▶ *The Very Hungry Caterpillar* by Eric Carle (Picture Puffins) may be a familiar story to the children, but it is one they enjoy hearing again and again. Use it as a stimulus before going on a bug hunt, or as reinforcement if you manage to find a caterpillar or two.
▶ Let the children use secondary sources to find out more about the life cycle of the butterfly or an animal that goes through a profound change, such as a frog. They could make a booklet for a class display.
▶ Find out as much as possible about the butterfly in the video. For instance, ask the children to find out where it lives and what it eats.
▶ Take the children out and look for 'baby' animals, such as caterpillars. Talk about the fact that all small animals are not necessarily baby animals. Look under leaves, stones, logs and so on. Back in the classroom, you could use the word cards on photocopiable page 33 to reinforce the learning about where you found the creatures, using words such as *under* and *next to*. Get the children to look in picture reference books for other creatures and their babies.
▶ Ask the children to find out more about a particular animal. They could focus, for example, on how many babies the creature might have at any one time, how it looks after the baby or babies, what the babies eat, and so on?

NOTES ON THE PHOTOCOPIABLE PAGES

Word cards PAGE 28

These word cards contain some of the basic vocabulary for the children to use and learn when learning about 'Plants and animals in the local environment'. They include:
▶ words relating to life processes
▶ words relating to animals
▶ words relating to plants
▶ words relating to scientific terms
▶ words relating to location.
Read through the word cards with the children. Check that the children understand all the words and clarify any that they don't.

Activities
▶ Ask the children to select a word card and to tell you what the word on it means.
▶ Ask the children to choose one of the plants or animals mentioned on the word cards and to write a poem about it.

Seed watch PAGE 34

This is a simple sheet for children to record the germination of their seeds on and the growth of the resultant seedlings. Cress seeds germinate and grow quickly, but French marigolds are also quick to germinate and can be grown on to provide colourful plants for the school garden.
Talk with the children about the things that are needed to help a seed germinate and grow. Explain that a seed needs warmth and water to germinate. Soil or compost gives the plant a firm anchor for its roots and supplies some nutrients so that it can grow into a healthy plant. When the children have filled in the first part of the sheet, ask them how long they think it will take for the seeds to germinate. Some seeds, especially those from trees, make take several weeks or even months. Some need to go through a cold winter before germinating the next spring. For reinforcement, once the sheets are completed, you could ask the children to cut out their finished pictures and sequence them on to a different sheet.

Life processes word cards

produce new plants

produce young

reproduce

eggs

caterpillar

chrysalis

Animals word cards (1)

spider

fly

bee

beetle

butterfly

caterpillar

snail

frog

robin

blackbird

sparrow

thrush

Plants word cards

daisy

dandelion

sunflower

oak tree

horse chestnut tree

apple tree

Scientific word cards

shoot
fruit
earth
table
root
leaf

Location word cards

under

within

inside

next to

outside

between

Seed watch

I planted my seed on _____

On _____ I saw the first shoot.

I watched it grow like this:

Date _____	Date _____
Date _____	Date _____

If I collected some seeds from my plant I could grow another

_____

VARIATION

Content and skills

This chapter links to Unit 2C 'Variation' of the QCA Scheme of Work for science at Key Stage 1. The Variation Resource Gallery on the CD-ROM, together with the teacher's notes and photocopiable pages in this chapter, can be used when teaching this unit.

As with the QCA Scheme of Work, this chapter helps children to learn about the similarities and differences between living things and to appreciate the wide variety of life. They will learn that living things can be grouped according to their similarities, even though they may, at first, look quite different. This is the beginning of classification.

The teacher's notes include ways of using the resources as a whole class, for group work or with individual children. Some of the activities suggested will link with other areas of the curriculum, such as English (by writing about their findings or making lists), maths (when they sort pictures of plants and animals) or art (when they make close observational drawings). Wherever possible, the activities encourage the children to ask questions and develop an enquiring approach to their learning.

Resources on the CD-ROM

There are photographs of plants and animals to illustrate the wide variety of living things. Photographs of people from different ethnic backgrounds help to show the variety found within the human race, and will enable you to discuss the similarities between living things as well as the differences. There are audio files on the CD-ROM which contain short passages of different animal sounds, again to illustrate the wide variety of sounds made by living things.

Photocopiable pages

The photocopiable pages in the book are also provided in PDF format on the CD-ROM and can be printed out from there. These include:
▶ word cards containing the essential vocabulary of the topic
▶ a story
▶ a writing frame.

Science skills

Skills such as observing, questioning, finding out, describing, sorting, sequencing, listening, speaking, reading, writing and drawing are involved in the activities suggested in the teacher's notes. For example, looking for similarities and differences between plants and animals will help develop the children's skills of observation. Thinking of words to describe animal movements will help to increase their vocabulary and encourage speaking and listening skills, as will talking about similarities and differences between families from different ethnic groups. Children will have the opportunity to practise sorting skills when grouping pictures of animals and plants.

NOTES ON THE CD-ROM RESOURCES

Dandelion diagram

This illustration of a dandelion plant shows the flower, stem, leaves, roots and seed head. Children should be familiar with the main parts of a plant from their work in Year 1. This work will help to consolidate that knowledge. It will also help children to understand that most plants have parts that are basically the same, even though they may look very different. This can be illustrated by looking at the 'Tree illustration' in the Variation Resource Gallery.

Discussing the illustration

▶ Show the children the illustration and ask if they know what sort of plant it shows.
▶ Ask the children to name the different parts of the dandelion plant. Can they say what the difference is between the flower head and the seed head? The flower head is yellow and fairly flat in shape. It has lots of little florets firmly fixed to the head of the plant. The seed head is round like a ball – it is white and fluffy. Each little seed has a 'parachute' attached to it and it comes away easily from the head of the plant. It is so light that it can be blown away on the wind.
▶ Ask if any of them have seen plants like this. Where did they see them? Was there just one plant or were there lots? Were they all exactly the same? Did they have mostly flowers or seed heads?
▶ Can anyone tell you what happens to the seeds? Explain how they are blown by the wind until they land and germinate if the ground is suitable.
▶ Discuss why the plant produces so many seeds. Tell the children that not all the seeds will find a suitable place to germinate and some may be eaten by small creatures
▶ Talk about why plants need roots. Describe how they help to hold the plant firmly in the ground and take up water and nutrients from it.

Activities

▶ Using the words from the 'Plant features word cards' (photocopiable page 42) ask individual children to come and add labels to the different parts of the plant on a large copy of the illustration.
▶ Bring a dandelion plant into the classroom and compare this with the illustration. Wash the plant and spread it out on a large sheet of paper. Then let the children add labels to it as appropriate, using the word cards on photocopiable page 42.
▶ Bring in another plant to compare the dandelion plant to, such as a daisy. Ask the children to tell you the similarities and the differences that they see. Children often find it easier to see differences and may need help to identify any similarities.
▶ Take the children out for a walk and look for other common plants. Encourage the children to collect any plants carefully and sensitively. Remind them to take only one specimen, but never to take a plant if there is only one present. Back in the classroom, use simple reference books to name any unknown plants that were collected. Remind the children to wash their hands after handling plants and soil.
▶ Ask the children to choose one of the plants found on the walk and make a detailed drawing of it. If the plant is complex it may be better to ask the children to concentrate on one part, such as the leaf or the flower, rather than attempting the whole plant.

Tree diagram

This is an illustration of a tree including flowers and roots. The tree is shown in its entiret,y including the roots to reinforce the children's understanding that trees are plants. The magnified inset shows that trees have flowers that develop into fruits. Use the illustration on its own or as part of a slideshow with the 'Dandelion illustration' in the Variation Resource Gallery in order to make comparisons between the two. Children will often tell you about differences between things but may need some encouragement to identify similarities. For example, they both have stems, although one is much thicker and tougher than the other. Both plants produce flowers and seeds, both have roots, and so on.

Photograph © Photodisc, Inc.

Discussing the illustration

▶ Look at the illustration of the tree and ask the children if they can name the different parts. Remind them that trees, too, are flowering plants, just like dandelions and daisies.

▶ Ask the children to tell you in what ways the tree is similar to a flowering plant like a dandelion. For example, they both have stems, although a tree's stem is called a *trunk*. They both have roots, leaves and flowers, and they both produce seeds.

▶ Ask the children to focus on how a tree is different from other plants, such as a dandelion. The tree is obviously much bigger than a dandelion. Talk about the hard, woody trunk of a tree compared to the softer, sappy stem of a dandelion. Point out that the tree would also produce many more flowers.

▶ Talk about how the roots of a tree would be correspondingly bigger in order to keep the plant stable during high winds and to take up the amount of water and nutrients that such a big plant needs.

Activities

▶ Use the 'Plant features word cards' on photocopiable page 42 to help the children to label the illustration. Ask the children, *Are the labels needed the same or different from those needed for the 'Dandelion illustration'?*

▶ Take the children out and look at any trees in the vicinity. Ask, *Are they all the same? If not, how can you tell they are different?*

▶ Compare a tree and a small plant. What about the size or the number of leaves? Do they both have the same size or number of flowers?

▶ Bring in some leaves from a small plant and some from a tree. Ask the children to compare the two types and ask them to describe how they feel. Encourage the children to think about how the trunks and twigs of trees are hard and woody, while smaller plants often have softer, juicier stalks.

▶ Let the children make a collection of different shaped leaves from a walk. They can press them and mount them on card so that they can be compared for size, shape, and so on. If these are covered in clear, sticky-backed plastic they will last for a considerable time, allowing the children to revisit the activity and consolidate their understanding.

▶ When you have collected and covered the leaves (see above), make sure there are at least two examples of each type of leaf and let the children play snap with the cards.

▶ Ask the children to compare two different leaves and to make lists of similarities and differences between them, such as *Both are green. One has a curvy edge and one has a spiky edge.* They could use the words on photocopiable page 44 to help them, such as *longer, similar to*.

Diagram of daisy plant showing roots

Children may be familiar with the parts of plants that they can see above ground, but may not always realise that roots are also an essential part of a plant even though they cannot see them. The daisy plant in the illustration has fine spreading roots, but some plants, such as carrots, parsnips or radishes, have a long fleshy taproot with small hair-like roots coming from it.

One or two potted plants would be useful to have when teaching this unit. The type will depend on the time of year. Pot chrysanthemums are available for most of the year. It might also be useful to have a carrot or parsnip to show the children. If this unit is being taught in the spring or early summer, bedding plants are readily available and relatively cheap.

Discussing the illustration

▶ Look at the illustration of the daisy plant and ask the children to name the different parts of it.

▶ Can the children tell you why any of the different parts are important? Remind them that flowers attract pollinating insects. Talk about the roots drawing up water and the leaves using sunshine to help the plant make its own food. (This is a simple introduction to work on photosynthesis that comes later in the children's science learning.)

▶ Stress the difference between a whole plant and parts of a plant.

Activities

▶ Take a small plant from its pot and wash the roots. Show it to the children so that they can compare this plant to the one in the illustration. Ask, *How is it similar? How is it different?*

▶ Ask the children to make a detailed drawing of the plant taken from its pot. If the plant is a complex one, talk about the features they should include in their drawings. The children could use the 'Plant features word cards' (photocopiable page 42) to help them label their drawing.
▶ Carefully re-pot the plant and encourage the children to help you take care of it. The roots must not be allowed to dry out during the previous activities if you wish to re-pot the plant.

SAME BUT DIFFERENT

White family, Afro-Caribbean family, Chinese family, Inuit family

This group of photographs shows families from different ethnic backgrounds. They demonstrate that people may have different features and skin colour while remaining essentially the same. Depending on the area in which you live, the children may have more or less experience of people from other races or cultures, so how you approach the teaching in these photographs will depend on the children's exposure to different cultures around them.

Discussing the photographs
▶ Look at each of the photographs and ask the children if they know any families or people like those shown in them
▶ Talk about the similarities between the families in the photographs. Ask, *Do all the people have the same number of eyes, limbs, ears? Are there grown ups and children in each family?*
▶ Then focus on the differences, asking *How are they different? Are all the people the same colour? Is their hair the same? How do their features differ? If the children were on different photographs could you match them to their own family?*
▶ Ask the children if they think everyone in the photographs has the same feelings. Ask, *What might make them happy or sad? Do you think they all sometimes get angry or cry?*

Activities
▶ Put the children into groups of four or five. Try and make the groups as varied as possible. Ask the children to look at the other people in their group and to make lists of similarities and differences between each other. For example, hair colour, eye colour, skin colour, number of arms, legs, eyes, ears, and so on.
▶ Group the children according to their birthdays. Are the children born in September always bigger than those born in June?
▶ Ask a child to describe the physical appearance of another child in the class, so that the rest of the class can guess who it is.
▶ Use face paints, false beards, wigs, hats, and so on, to disguise the children. Can their classmates still recognise them? Which parts are not easy to change or disguise? For example, the way they walk, their voice, the colour of their eyes.
▶ Get the children to make masks for a masked ball. How easy is it for them to find their friends when they have their masks on?

DIFFERENT ANIMALS AND PLANTS

Human, Bee, Spider, Worm, Mealworms, Snail, Dog, Horse, Bird, Snake, Crocodile, Butterfly, Whale, Grass, Ivy, Holly bush, Cherry tree, Daffodil, Oak tree

This collection of photographs helps demonstrate the wide variety of living things in both the animal and plant kingdoms. The children need to understand that animals and plants are all living organisms and need to grow and reproduce. Both need water in order to survive, but plants are able to make their own 'food' in order to produce more plant material, while animals, ultimately, depend on plants for their food. Most animals can move from place to place and make some sort of noise. Plants do often move in response to a stimulus, such as flowers openingwhen the sun shines or growing towards a light source, but they are usually rooted in one place and do not make noises.You may find it worthwhile printing each photograph out, mounting it on card and covering it with sticky-backed plastic to make a durable resource for the children to handle and play games with.

Discussing the photographs

▶ Remind the children that living things are broadly divided into two groups – animals and plants.

▶ Look at each photograph and ask the children to tell you whether the organism is a plant or an animal. How do they know? Encourage them to tell you their ideas, such as animals move, plants have leaves, animals eat, and so on.

▶ Ask the children how they know that humans are part of the animal kingdom. Talk about how we move, that we need to eat and drink and that we have babies (reproduce).

▶ Make a slideshow of all the animal photographs and talk about how they are similar or different. For example, the worm, the mealworms, the snail, the whale and the snake are all animals, but they don't have legs. They all have to feed and breathe and they all have babies (reproduce).

▶ Similarly, with the pictures of plants. They all have roots and they all produce flowers and seeds. The daffodil dies down each year and the oak tree loses its leaves, but the holly keeps its leaves all year round.

Activities

▶ Give groups of children copies of the photographs and ask them to sort them into animals and plants.

▶ Choose one plant and one animal and ask the children to compare the two. Make a list on the board of the simple characteristics of each, such as the spider has eight legs, the tree has no legs; the tree has flowers and seeds, the spider lays eggs that hatch into baby spiders; the spider eats flies, the tree does not eat.

▶ Choose two animals, such as the bird and the snake, and ask the children to make comparisons between them. Use questions to prompt their thinking, such as *Do they have the same number of legs? Does one have a shell? Where are the eyes?*

▶ Compare two plants, such as the ivy and the holly bush, in the same way. Look at the shape of the leaves, the size and characteristics of the plants, and so on.

▶ Give the children a copy of the word cards on photocopiable pages 42 and 43, and different animal and plant photographs, asking them to choose appropriate words to label their photograph with, such as *shell*, *fur*, *stem*, *leaves*.

TREES HAVE FLOWERS TOO

Cherry tree in bloom, Hazel catkins, Pussy willow

Most trees flower in the spring, so, if you are doing this unit in the spring, take the children out to look for any trees that are flowering in the vicinity. Some trees, such as oak and sycamore, have long green/yellow catkin-like flowers that may be difficult to see at first glance. The flowers on a cherry tree are usually much more visible, and these blossom-laden trees are often quite spectacular when in full bloom. Encourage the children to look carefully and describe what they see.

Hazel catkins are often the first sign of spring in February and March. If the catkins are gently shaken it is possible to see clouds of pollen being shed from each one They are really the male parts of the plant and separate from the female flower, which is a very small, red, rather insignificant structure on the stem. Pussy willow develops a coating of yellow pollen produced by the male anthers as it matures. The catkin is actually made up of many tiny florets that can be seen as the catkins develop. When ripe, the seeds develop a hairy 'parachute' that allows them to be carried away on the wind, rather like dandelion seeds.

Discussing the photographs

▶ Remind the children that trees, too, are flowering plants. Look carefully at the photograph and ask the children if they can see the flowers.

▶ Look at the photographs of the hazel catkins and pussy willow. Talk about how some trees, such as hazel or some willows, flower very early in the spring before they have any leaves. This is because they rely on the wind to blow their pollen from flower to flower. Any leaves would get in the way and make pollination more difficult.

Photograph © Nova Developments

Activities
▶ Take the children on a walk to look for flowering trees. Are the flowers always easy to see? Are they always the same colour, shape, and so on?
▶ 'Adopt' a flowering tree near the school and visit it at regular interval to watch the flowers die and the fruits form. An apple tree or horse chestnut is good to watch if you have one nearby.
▶ Bring in some catkins (in the spring) and let the children use a hand lens to look for the tiny flowers. The long catkins are the male flowers producing lots of pollen. The female flowers are very small and often tucked away in the joints of the twigs.
▶ Let the children use old gardening magazines or catalogues to find pictures of other flowering trees.

ANIMAL SOUNDS

Human voices, Sheep, Seagulls

There is a huge range of sounds made by animals, some of which are inaudible to the human ear, for example the sound made by bats as part of their echo location system. Humans use words or calls to communicate with each other, but other creatures also use sounds to communicate. Some of the sounds may serve as recognition signals, others may signal fear, anger or pleasure. We sometimes use sounds to identify animals, such as birds, that can be difficult to actually see.

Most children should have heard the sounds included here and will be familiar with a range of human voices. They will recognise the different tones that can indicate pleasure, anger, fright, and so on. They will also have learned to recognise specific people by the sound of their voice. Similarly, a sheep may recognise the bleating of its lamb, and vice versa, so that they may find each other in the flock. Bird calls are made for reasons, such as marking a territory, attracting a mate, alerting others to danger, and so on. The seagull has a very distinctive call and may be heard in the countryside, following a plough or on rubbish tips, as well as at the seaside.

Discussing the sounds
▶ Talk about why animals make sounds and explain that it is one way in which animals communicate with each other.
▶ Discuss the sorts of things that animals may be communicating For example, they may be announcing that they have possession of a particular territory and are warning others to keep off. They may be showing off in order to attract a mate. They may be warning others in their group that they have found a good source of food or that there is danger approaching.
▶ Play the audio clips to the children and ask what they indicate. For example, there are lots of people chattering and laughing in the 'Human voices' audio clip. Ask the children, *Are they enjoying themselves? Where might they be? What might they be talking about?*
▶ Discuss the different sounds on the 'Sheep' audio clip. Ask the children if they can tell the difference between the sheep and the lambs. Discuss how they may be using sound to identify each other in a large flock.
▶ Talk about the 'Seagulls' clip and how they may be using their calls to mark their territories and warn other birds to keep off, or how they might be looking for a mate or warning of some danger.

Activities
▶ Use the photocopiable page 'Squeaking and roaring' (page 48) for the children to match the animal to the sound it makes.
▶ In groups, ask the children to research what sorts of sounds are made by other creatures. Make a class collection of words that describe animal sounds, such as *grunt, meow, twitter, neigh, bark, bleat* and *moo*.
▶ Sing 'Old MacDonald had a farm' together, making the sounds of animals the children suggest.
▶ Divide the class in half and sit them with their backs to each other. Alternatively, you could hide half the class behind a screen instead. Ask a child from one half of the class to speak and the children in the other half to guess who it is. Can the children describe how they know who is speaking?

NOTES ON THE PHOTOCOPIABLE PAGES

Word cards
PAGE 42

These word cards contain some of the basic vocabulary for the children to use and learn when learning about the variation in living things. These include:
▶ words relating to plant features
▶ words relating to animal features
▶ words relating to comparing
▶ words relating to generalising.
Read through the words with the children and ask which words they have heard before. Are there any words they don't understand?

Activities
▶ Cut the words out and spread them on a table. Ask the children to find specific words.
▶ Use the words as a word bank to help the children label pictures or to help them with their writing when learning about this unit.

The tortoise and the hare
PAGE 46

Use the story to reinforce the children's understanding about the similarities and differences between animals. For example, the tortoise and the hare both have four legs, two eyes and two ears. The hare's ears are very prominent, but those of the tortoise are hardly visible. The tortoise carries a shell in which to shelter, but the hare is covered in fur. The tortoise moves very slowly and can retreat into its shell if danger threatens, whereas the hare uses its speed to run away.

Discussing the story
▶ Read the story to the children. Talk about the similarities and differences in the way in which the two animals move.
▶ Ask the children why they think a hare moves quickly, while a tortoise is so slow. Talk about how the hare needs to run away from predators, while the tortoise can hide inside its shell and, therefore, does not need to move quickly when predators are around.
▶ Discuss the fact that we all have strengths and weaknesses and may not all be good at the same thing, but it is always important to do our best at whatever we attempt.

Activities
▶ Make a list of animals that move slowly. Ask, *How do they protect themselves instead of running away?* For example, a slow-moving snail can retreat into its shell; a sloth lives high in the trees out of danger.
▶ Discuss why some animals need to be able to move very quickly. As a class, or in smaller groups, get the children to work together to write a sentence that explains why.
▶ Use the photographs from 'Different animals and plants' in the Variation Resource Gallery and look for similarities and differences between them. Prompt the children by asking, *Have they all got ears and eyes? Are they all the same shape? Can they all run? Have any of them got their own protection from danger like the tortoise?*

Squeaking and roaring
PAGE 48

This is a fun way for children to think about the many different sorts of sounds that animals make. Children will simply need to draw a line to match the animal to the sound it makes. The sheet provides a great opportunity to discuss the variety of sounds made by animals, including sounds that some animals make that are too high for humans to hear, for example, bats. Talk to the children about why animals make sounds and how different sounds are used for attracting a mate, proclaiming territory, warning of danger, and so on. This sheet is a good companion to the 'Animal sounds' in the Variation Resource Gallery.

Photograph © Ingram Publishing

Plant features word cards

flower

stem

leaves

roots

seed head

branch

trunk

Animal features word cards

feathers
fur
shell
fins
beak
wings

Comparative word cards

long

longer

longest

similar to

different from

Generalisation word cards

most have

we all

everyone

some

few

many

The tortoise and the hare

In the mountainous lands of a wonderful country there lived a hare. He frolicked among the wild flowers, fields and hedges of his home. He galloped about, dashing here and there, wanting to know everything that was going on. Not very far away there lived a tortoise. He had made his home beside a stream. He sat about all day inside his own basin-like shell that suited him very well. It served him as shelter and protection. Now and then he would poke his head and legs out of his shell and take a very slow walk, but not for long. For most of the time he was tucked away inside his shell, seemingly asleep.

The two animals had never met until one day the tortoise put his head out of his shell and saw the bright eyes of the hare staring at him. The hare laughed out loud.

"It is rude to laugh at people, Mr Hare," said the tortoise with dignity. "Why are you laughing?"

"Because you are such a peculiar looking creature," replied the hare, "and you've no legs at all."

The tortoise proved that this was not true by sticking his legs out of his shell. "Run a race with me," he challenged the hare, "then you will see that I have perfectly good legs."

This made the hare laugh even more. "Run a race with you? I certainly will," he said. "Where shall we race?"

"Wherever you like," snapped the tortoise, now thoroughly cross.

They asked Mr Fox to be the referee and to map out the course. Mr Fox asked what the prize would be, hoping to be asked to hold it. The tortoise replied that there was no prize, but that they were going to race for honour and glory. Mr Fox was disappointed, but agreed to mark out the course.

"The longer and harder you make it the better," said the tortoise.

The fox looked all around for a suitable course and saw a city miles and miles away. "You can race from here to that city," he said. "Leave that hill to the left and cross the river on the right and then go straight through the valley and the wood. I shall keep a sharp eye on you both to see fair play."

"Ready, steady, go!" called Mr Fox.

"Goodbye," said Mr Hare. "I'll wait for you when I get there. See you in a day or two."

■■SCHOLASTIC
PHOTOCOPIABLE

The hare bounded happily off down the path on his long powerful back legs in the direction of the distant city. He pranced along, laughing to himself. He was sure that the slow old tortoise would be a very long time plodding along the course. Why, he might never reach the city at all. The tortoise took his time, pushing his legs as far out as they would go, straightening them as best he could to take the weight of his large shell, and then he set off in the same direction.

The hare galloped and hopped merrily along on his long, powerful legs for a mile or so and then, feeling a little tired, he settled in the shade of a beautiful crab apple tree to rest. He found a most comfortable spot and lay down, his long ears drooping and his short tail resting on the ground.

"It will be all right if I sleep for the rest of the day," he told himself. "That slow old tortoise with his stubby legs and heavy shell will never catch up with me." He settled himself with his nose on the soft fur of his front feet and fell deeply asleep.

The tortoise, under his heavy shell was more wide-awake than he had ever been in his life! He did not feel the brambles through his tough, scaly skin and he swam the river with ease in spite of his cumbersome shell. Slowly and surely, surely and slowly, he made his way along the course, concentrating on putting one foot in front of the other, and not stopping for anything. When evening came he saw the spires of the city in front of him.

The hare slept soundly all day long. When the evening came he woke with a start. The sun had set and he could see the moon.

"Oh dear, I've slept longer than I meant to," he said to himself. "Never mind, if I run as fast as I can, and that is very fast indeed, I should still beat that slow old tortoise." He leapt to his feet and rushed off as fast as the wind.

Down the hill he went. He swam the river with fast, strong strokes of his powerful, furry legs, galloped over the hill and through the woods until at last he saw the city spires in front of him. But disaster! When he reached the city gates what do you think he saw? Yes! He saw Mr Tortoise, accompanied by Mr Fox, taking a well-earned rest!

"Ah-ha!" shouted Mr Fox as Mr Hare sat down exhausted and shook his long ears angrily. "You may be a very quick runner, and I know you are because I have tried to catch you many times in order to eat you, but if quick runners want to beat slow runners they must not lie down and sleep on the way!"

Photograph © Ingram Publishing

Squeaking and roaring

▷ Draw a line from each animal to the noise it makes.

lion	oink
mouse	moo
horse	neigh
bird	baa
cow	twitter
pig	squeak
human	cluck
sheep	croak
chicken	roar
frog	talk

GROUPING AND CHANGING MATERIALS

Content and skills

This chapter links to Unit 2D 'Grouping and changing materials' of the QCA Scheme of Work for science at Key Stage 1. The Grouping and Changing Materials Resource Gallery on the CD-ROM, together with the teacher's notes and photocopiable pages in this chapter, can be used in teaching this unit.

This chapter helps children to identify a range of materials and to learn more about them. For example, that some occur naturally and that these natural materials can be used to make objects by such processes as cutting, shaping and polishing. They also learn that some materials are manufactured and can be changed by heat, producing a new, useful material. For example, in cooking the ingredients to make a cake, making glass or firing clay to change it into a vessel that will hold water.

The teacher's notes include ways of using the resources as a whole class, for group work or as individuals. Some of the activities suggested will link with other areas of the curriculum, such as English, maths or art. Wherever possible, the activities encourage the children to ask questions and develop an enquiring approach to their learning.

Resources on the CD-ROM

Children obviously need to handle and feel materials in a practical way, but the photographs on the CD-ROM can be used to introduce, reinforce and enhance the children's learning. There are pictures of a range of naturally occurring and manufactured materials and some objects made from them. A video clip shows materials being changed into objects and what the application of heat does to a material. Teacher's notes are provided in the accompanying book, containing background information and suggesting ways to use the resources in teaching the children.

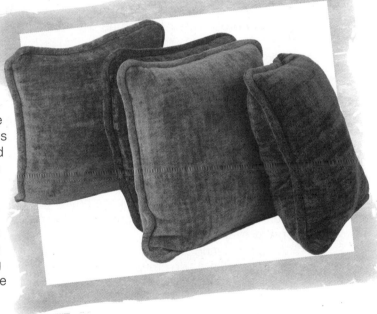

Photocopiable pages

The photocopiable pages in the book are also provided in PDF format on the CD-ROM and can be printed out from there. They include:
▶ word cards containing essential vocabulary
▶ an information sheet.

Science skills

The resources on the CD-ROM and the activities suggested to deliver these resources to the children in the book focus on bringing out skills, such as observing, questioning, finding out, describing, sorting, sequencing, investigating, listening, speaking, reading, writing and drawing. For example, children are encouraged to to recognise and name a range of naturally occurring materials, to distinguish between a material and the object it is made into, to describe the effect of heat on some materials and how they are changed as a result. Children's natural curiosity can be encouraged by questions such as *How can we find out? What would happen if…? Why do you think…?* At this stage children may need help in formulating initial questions, but will soon be full of ideas once an enquiry is underway.

NOTES ON THE CD-ROM RESOURCES

RAW MATERIALS

Slice of tree trunk, Cotton bolls, Goat's wool, Lump of clay, Plastic granules

These photographs show different materials, both manufactured and naturally occurring materials. Children will be familiar with objects that have been made from the materials in the photographs, but may not have seen the raw materials before.

Children need to be able to distinguish between naturally occurring and manufactured materials and know that they are used for different purposes according to their properties. At this stage children only need to know about simple properties of materials, such as we use wool for clothes because it is warm, or wood can be shaped and joined relatively easily. They build on this knowledge later on in Key Stage 2.

Discussing the photographs

▶ Look at the photographs with the children. Ask if they can identify the objects in them.
▶ Talk about the fact that some materials occur naturally and can be turned into objects by such processes as cutting, joining, shaping. For example, wood can be made into things like spoons, bowls and chairs. Wool from sheep or goats can be spun and then knitted, either by a person or a machine, into jumpers or scarves.
▶ Tell the children that natural materials either grow, such as wool or wood, or can be found almost ready to use, such as clay. Manufactured materials are those that have to go through a profound process (such as crude oil) in order to turn them into commonly used materials, such as plastic.
▶ Help the children to make comparisons between naturally occurring materials and materials that are manufactured. For example, the raw materials that are made into plastic or glass have to go through a profound manufacturing process involving heat in order to change them into a new, more useful material.
▶ Remind the children that it is not only fabrics that are materials, but that everything is a material.

Activities

▶ Ask the children to say whether each of the materials in the photographs is natural or manufactured. Make lists under the headings *Natural* and *Manufactured* on the board. How do the children know which group to put the materials into? Ask the children to add their own examples to the lists.
▶ Make a collection of small pieces of naturally occurring and manufactured materials for the children to sort into two groups. Provide things made from glass, plastic, metal, leather, cotton, wool (beware – if you are using sheep's wool, it must be washed before the children handle it), wood, and so on. Make sure that any glass you give the children to handle has no sharp edges and cannot be broken (the small, coloured and clear nuggets of glass that are found in craft shops or large glass beads are suitable). Talk to the children about why they have sorted the materials into a particular group. How did they decide which ones are natural and which ones are manufactured?
▶ Give the children copies of the word cards on photocopiable pages 54 and 55 to label the collection of natural and manufactured items with. This will help familiarise them with words such as *wool*, *glass*, *clay*.
▶ Let the children make a class collage of natural materials and one of manufactured materials. (It can be useful to draw large landscapes for the children to collage into.)

Photograph © Nova Developments

MADE FROM…

Wooden chair, Cotton T-shirt, Woollen hat and scarf, Clay flowerpots, Plastic bucket

It is often difficult for children to recognise a raw material for what it is when it has been made into something else. It is useful to compare the natural material with the object made from it. Re-use the photographs from 'Raw materials' above to match with these 'made' objects. Plastic is sometimes made to mimic a natural material so closely that even adults have difficulty distinguishing it from the real thing.

Discussing the photographs

▶ Look at each photograph and ask the children if they can identify the object and the material it is made from.

▶ Talk about the fact that some of the objects have been made from naturally occurring materials and that these have been cut and shaped, knitted or woven. For instance, the T-shirt has been woven from cotton which has been spun into yarn from the raw fibre. This raw fibre has been harvested from the cotton plant.

▶ Tell the children that manufactured objects, such as the plastic bucket, have to go through a manufacturing process where the original raw materials are mixed, heated and poured into moulds, a process that changes the original material.

Activities

▶ Make a slideshow of the photographs from 'Raw materials' above and ask the children to match these 'Made from…' photographs with their original raw material.

▶ Get the children to label the photographs using the 'Materials word cards' on photocopiable pages 54 and 55. They could also add word card labels to identify the photographs as being made from natural or manufactured resources.

▶ Bring in a collection of raw materials and objects made from them. Ask the children to sort and label these and to tell you how they decided to sort and label them.

▶ Look around the classroom. How many things can the children identify that have been made from manufactured materials and how many from natural materials? Are there more of one than the other? Talk to the children about why this might be. For example, it might be cheaper and easier to make a chair out of plastic than from wood or metal, or that plastic chairs are lighter and easier to move around.

▶ Take the children on a walk around the school, both inside and out, and identify materials and objects, natural and manufactured, that have been used to build the school, the furniture and the playground. Discuss with the children some of the reasons for using natural or manufactured materials to make these things from.

▶ Give the children some raw clay to handle and to make small thumb pots with. Ask them to predict what will happen to their pots if they are put into a kiln and fired. (The clay is changed so that adding water to it will not make it soft again.) Fire the children's pots if possible and look at them again. Talk about how the heat of the kiln has changed them.

▶ Use the information sheet 'The history of paper' (photocopiable page 58) with the children to reinforce their understanding of raw and manufactured materials.

▶ Read the story of Pinocchio to the children to illustrate things being made from wood.

Video: Making glass bottles

Glass is manufactured from a range of naturally occurring materials that are changed profoundly by the application of heat. During this process a new material is formed. This is a chemical change that cannot be reversed, although children do not need to know this at this stage. Obsidian is a type of glass that is sometimes produced by the application of heat during a volcanic eruption.

Discussing the video

▶ Watch the video with the children and ask them to tell you what material is involved. Then ask them to look particularly at what is happening to the glass as the bottles are made.

▶ Tell the children that by heating sand and other materials a new material – glass – has been made.

► Talk about the fact that people have been making glass for thousands of years. The ancient Egyptians made glass in 2000BC.
► Talk about some of the things the children know that are made from glass.
► Talk about the various stages shown in the video that are needed to make the glass bottles.
► Talk about how the glass is formed into a shape while it is still hot and liquid and that once it cools it becomes hard and keeps its shape.

Activities
► Ask the children to draw a series of pictures representing what they have seen on the video for a class display.
► Ask the children to write a short piece on how glass is made. They could use words such as *cool* or *melt* on phocopiable page 57 to help them.
► Put out dry sand and glass nuggets or beads in separate trays for the children to handle and compare. Make sure they understand the fact that sand is the major ingredient of glass.
► Show the children, and talk about, a collection of objects made from glass. (Safety tip – do not allow the children to handle them.) Try and have as wide a variety of objects as possible so that the children appreciate the wide range of things that can be made from glass, from windows to ornaments.
► Watch the video again and ask the children to suggest as many descriptive words as they can about the manufacturing processes. Make a list on the board of their suggestions. The children could then use a combination of these words, and those on photocopiable pages 56 and 57, to write 'glassy' poems.
► Write a class leaflet to inform others about how sand is turned into glass bottles and other things.

NOTES ON THE PHOTOCOPIABLE PAGES

Word cards  PAGE 54

These word cards contain some of the basic vocabulary for the children to use and learn when learning about 'Grouping and changing materials'. They include:
► words relating to materials
► words relating to changing materials.
Read through the word cards with the children. Make sure the children know what the words mean and help them with any words they don't understand.

Activities
► Print all the word cards out and ask the children to find specific words.
► Ask the children to select several cards and tell you what the words on them mean.
They could add the words to their personal dictionaries.

The history of paper PAGE 58

This information text provides a simple outline of the history of papermaking. It details that not all paper is made from wood pulp and that different materials have been used through the centuries. Use it as a basis for finding out more about how paper is manufactured today.

Discussing the text
► Read the information sheet through with the children and make sure that they understand it.
► Ask the children to tell you what the raw material in papermaking is.
► Talk about the fact that not all paper is made from wood. Other naturally occurring materials, such as flax, can be used to make linen paper.
► Discuss the different uses of paper, including packing and parcelling, for writing on, making plates and cups and even toilet paper!
► Ask the children if they think that they ever go through a day without using paper in some form or other. Remind them how important paper is in our lives.

Photograph © Ingram Publishing

Activities

▶ Ask the children to use the Internet and/or other secondary sources to add any information about paper they can find to the sheet, including papermaking today.

▶ Get the children to write a poem about a fun use of paper, for example party streamers or wrapping paper.

▶ Collect as wide a range of papers and card as possible for the children to handle and to collage pictures with. Try to include some papers that can be torn easily and some that the children will have to cut. For example, linen paper, card, tissue, and so on.

▶ Ask the children to think of as many different ways in which we use paper and card as they can. Make a list on a large piece of paper with plenty of spare space on it. It could then be pinned up in the classroom for the children to add to every time they think of a new use of paper.

▶ Set the children a range of tasks involving the use of paper, such as writing a short letter, making a greeting card, wrapping a parcel, drying their hands, painting a picture, making paper chains, and so on. Ask them to select a paper that is suitable for the job from a range that you have collected.

▶ Let the children make and decorate paper beads to thread on to strings. Show them how to put torn tissue into a solution of cellulose paste to soak. (Beware – do not use wallpaper paste as this usually contains a fungicide.) Roll lumps of the soaked tissue into balls about the size of a large marble and set aside to dry. When dry, use needles and thread from the sewing equipment to thread the beads on to strings. They can then paint and decorate them. This is a messy activity, but fun! The children could make strings of ten beads to hang up in the classroom to use as a counting aid.

▶ Ask the children to keep a tally sheet for 24 hours, making a mark every time they use paper or card for any purpose. Discuss which type of paper they used most often. Talk about how essential paper is to us in today's world.

Photograph © Stockbyte

wood

metal

leather

wool

Materials word cards (2)

cotton

plastic

clay

glass

paper

Changing materials word cards (1)

squash

bend

twist

stretch

Changing materials word cards (2)

heat

cool

freeze

melt

boil

The history of paper

Using paper for writing on goes back a long way. It wasn't until paper was invented that people could pass on written information easily and cheaply. Before that, people chipped away at stone, or used things like waxed boards or clay tablets to record information on.

Paper gets its name from *papyrus* which was invented by the Ancient Egyptians about 4000BC. That is 6000 years ago! It was made of woven and pounded reeds. About AD105, the Chinese developed a paper that looked more like paper looks today. This was made from pulped fishing nets. Later on, people also used a surface for writing on called *parchment* or *vellum*, which was made from animal skins.

It took a long time for paper to come to Europe and we did not start making our own paper in this country until about 1500. Now we would find it difficult to manage without it.

Today, paper is mostly made from wood pulp and recycled paper. Most of the wood pulp that we use comes from managed pine forests where new trees are planted to replace those that are cut down for papermaking. When paper is recycled it is cleaned, pulped and used again.

Paper now comes in many, many different forms and is used for a huge range of different purposes, not just for writing on. For example, packing and wrapping, mopping up and wiping.

FORCES AND MOVEMENT

Content and skills

This chapter links to Unit 2E 'Forces and movement' of the QCA Scheme of Work for science at Key Stage 1. The Forces and Movement Resource Gallery on the CD-ROM, together with the teacher's notes and photocopiable pages in this chapter, can be used when teaching this unit.

As with the QCA Scheme of Work, this chapter encourages children to think about the concept of forces and movement and how pushes and pulls can make things move, slow down, speed up and change direction or shape. It builds on the work done in Year 1, in QCA Unit 1E 'Pushes and pulls'.

The teacher's notes include ways of using the resources as a whole class, for group work or with individual children. Some of the activities suggested will link with other areas of the curriculum, such as English, maths or art. Wherever possible, the activities encourage the children to ask questions and develop an enquiring approach to their learning.

Resources on the CD-ROM

The CD-ROM contains photographs of objects that can be moved by pushes and pulls, and objects whose direction and speed can be changed by exerting a force on them. Video clips show a child engaged in exerting a pushing and pulling force on bicycle pedals and a child being pushed and pulled on a swing in order to create movement.

Photocopiable pages

The photocopiable pages in the book are also provided in PDF format on the CD-ROM and can be printed out from there. They include:
▶ word cards containing the essential vocabulary of the topic
▶ a poem
▶ information text
▶ a writing frame.

Science skills

Skills such as observing, questioning, describing, finding out, sorting, sequencing, listening, speaking – including saying what is expected to happen – reading, writing and drawing are involved in the activities suggested in the teacher's notes in this chapter. For example, looking closely at the video clips and naming the forces, such as pushes or pulls, needed to move the objects will help children understand that a force of some kind is needed to make things move. Saying what they expect to happen and then finding out what does happen to the speed and direction of a ball when it is hit with a bat will encourage children to make predictions and then carry out a simple investigation.

Photograph © Ross Whitaker/SODA

NOTES ON THE CD-ROM RESOURCES

TOYS

Doll's pushchair, Bike, Bat and ball, Swing, Ice skates

Children need to understand that a force is needed to make things move, stop, start, speed up, slow down or change direction or shape. Most forces are either a push or a pull. (A twist is a push and a pull combined.) You could use the information sheet 'What forces are and what they do' on photocopiable page 69 for support if required.

Discussing the photographs

▶ Remind the children that a force is needed to make things move and that this is usually a push or a pull.

▶ Talk about what forces are and what they do in simple terms.

▶ After looking at each photograph, ask the children to tell you whether the object is being pushed or pulled to make it move. The pushchair is usually pushed, but could be pulled. The bike is moved by pushing down on the pedals. The ball is pushed as it is thrown and pushed again by the bat, which changes its direction. Discuss the fact that a swing can be moved by being pulled back or pushed forward. The person wearing the ice skates pushes against the ice to move forward, but the ice is slippery so that the skates move over it easily.

▶ Talk about the difference between pushes and pulls. For example, cyclists often wear clamps that clamp their foot to the pedals so that they can pull up on them as well as pushing down and thus exert a force for longer in order to make the bike go faster.

Activities

▶ Give the children copies of the information sheet 'What forces are and what they do'. Read this through with them to reinforce their understanding of forces.

▶ Use work with the small apparatus in PE to extend the children's experience of using forces to make things move, speed up, slow down and change direction. Discuss each activity with the children and ask them whether a push or a pull is being used in the following activities:

Bat and ball: In pairs, get one child to throw a ball (a push starts the ball moving) for their partner to bat away (another push that speeds the ball up and changes the direction in which it is travelling).

Beanbag: In pairs, get one child to throw a beanbag to their partner (a push) who should catch the beanbag and this stops it moving.

Skipping rope: Children could turn the rope and skip with it (a pull and a push); jump over a moving rope (a push off the ground); have a tug of war (pulls).

▶ Ask the children to choose one of the small apparatus activities they performed and draw a picture to show themselves doing the activity. Ask them to label it with the appropriate forces words. Let them use the word cards on photocopiable page 65 to help. For example, a picture of a child throwing a ball should be labelled *push*; children having a tug o' war should be labelled *pull*.

▶ Ask a child who has roller skates to bring them in and demonstrate how they skate. Ask the other children to use forces vocabulary to talk about what is happening as the skates move. For example, the person skating is pushing against the ground to make the wheels go round. If they stop pushing they stop moving forward.

▶ Push one roller skate (minus child!) and see how far it travels. Measure the distance. Ask the children what will happen if the skate is pushed harder. Push the skate harder and test the children's predictions. Measure the distance again.

▶ Organise the children into groups and give each group a toy car. Ask them to perform the same test as above. Make sure that each child in the group has a turn at pushing the car and get the children to measure the distance the car travels each time. Look at the children's results within each group. Are the distances travelled the same? If not, why not? Talk about how they could make the test fair and make the push the same each time (by using a ramp at different levels and starting the car the same place on the ramp each time and running it on to the same surface).

▶ Make a collection of small-wheeled toys that are moved by pushes or pulls. Ask the children to group them according to whether they are pushed or pulled in order to make them move.

▶ Let the children make different wheeled models from construction kits.

▶ Bring a bike into school for the children to look at and discuss how it works in terms of forces and pushes and pulls.

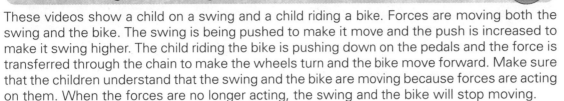

Video: Moving (1), Moving (2)

These videos show a child on a swing and a child riding a bike. Forces are moving both the swing and the bike. The swing is being pushed to make it move and the push is increased to make it swing higher. The child riding the bike is pushing down on the pedals and the force is transferred through the chain to make the wheels turn and the bike move forward. Make sure that the children understand that the swing and the bike are moving because forces are acting on them. When the forces are no longer acting, the swing and the bike will stop moving.

Discussing the video

▶ Show the children the video of the child on the swing (Moving 2) and ask them to look carefully, noting especially the way in which the swing is moved. Ask, *Does it need to be pushed or pulled?*

▶ Look at how the swing is started. Note that to start the swing it is being pulled before it is pushed. Ask the children if they can see how the movement is stopped. (The swing is pulled back by the adult to stop it moving forward again.)

▶ Can the children suggest how the swing can be made to go higher?

▶ Watch the video of the boy riding his bike (Moving 1). Discuss how he makes the bike move. Ensure that the children realise that he is pushing down on the pedals.

▶ Again, look at how the boy starts the bike moving and how he stops it.

▶ Talk about how the boy could make the bike speed up and slow down.

▶ Ask the children to think of other things that are moved by a push or a pull. Talk to the children about the fact that a force is needed to make anything move, such as pulling a drawer open or turning on a tap (explain that a twist is both a push and a pull).

Activities

▶ Take the children to a playground if possible, or talk about playground apparatus, to investigate using a force to make things move. Identify the forces used as pushes or pulls in the different apparatus.

▶ Read the children the RL Stevenson poem 'The Swing' (photocopiable page 68) and talk about the pushes and pulls a swing needs to move.

▶ Borrow a trolley from Reception and ask the children to find out whether a full or empty trolley is easier or harder to move. Use a force meter to measure the force needed to pull it. Remind the children that they need to take their measurement when the trolley is rolling. (When the initial inertia has been overcome.)

▶ Make a collection of pictures of objects that are moved by a pull, push or twist and paste them on to card to make playing cards. Do the same with copies of the 'Forces word cards' (photocopiable page 65). Lay the cards face down on a table in two separate groups. Ask the children to turn the cards over two at a time (one from each group). If their object is one that is pulled and their word is *pull*, they can keep the pair. If not, the cards are turned over again. The child with the most pairs at the end of the game is the winner.

▶ Give the children a copy of the 'Push, pull or twist' sheet (photocopiable page 70) to record things at home that are pushed, pulled or twisted. Make a list on the board of the children's findings or ideas. Make sure they have included such things as taps or doorknobs that are twisted (a push and a pull).

▶ As a class, use found materials to make a model playground. Use copies of the 'Forces word cards' (photocopiable page 65) to label whether the playground objects need a push or pull to make them move. Encourage the children to think about how the objects move and use the 'Movement word cards' (photocopiable pages 63 and 64) to prompt them to think of what makes things *speed up* or *change direction*.

Photograph © Ingram Publishing

NOTES ON THE PHOTOCOPIABLE PAGES

Word cards
PAGE 63

These word cards contain some of the basic vocabulary for the children to use and learn when learning about 'Forces and movement'. These include:
► words relating to movement
► words relating to forces
► words relating to comparing movement.
Read through the words with the children. Ask which words the children have heard before. Are there any words they don't understand?

Activities
► Let the children write the words in their personal dictionaries.
► Spread the word cards out on a table and ask the children to find specific words.

The Swing
PAGE 68

This poem by Robert Louis Stevenson can be used to reinforce a discussion about the pushes and pulls a swing needs to make it move, go higher and stop.

Discussing the poem
► Ask if any of the children have ever been on a swing. What did it feel like? Did they need help to get the swing moving?
► Talk about how a swing is made to move, how it is pushed forward and pulled back.
► Ask the children if they go higher on a swing if they are pushed harder?
► Talk about what the children could see when they were on a swing.

Activities
► Ask the children to write their own poems about being on a swing.
► Get the class to paint pictures of children on swings and to write labels about the forces involved.
► Read the poem again while the children watch the video and then discuss the movement of the swing in terms of forces. Discuss how the swing would need to be pushed harder to get it high in the sky so that they could see over the fields and the garden wall.

What forces are and what they do
PAGE 69

This information text gives simple definitions of forces and how they work. It may be useful when talking about forces with the children, or as a reminder for them as they work through the topic.

Push, pull or twist
PAGE 70

Use this sheet to help children to find and list things at home that need a push, pull or twist to make them move or work. Remind them about what they have learned and ask them to give you some examples of push, pull or twist forces before they take the sheet home. Read through the sheet and make sure that they understand what they need to do to complete it. When the children bring their sheets back to school, talk about some of the things they have listed. Has anyone found anything unusual?

Movement word cards (1)

direction

distance

force

change direction

backwards

forwards

Movement word cards (2)

speed up

slow down

start

stop

turn

Forces word cards

push

pull

twist

bend

squeeze

stretch

Comparative word cards (1)

fast

faster

fastest

slow

slower

slowest

Comparative word cards (2)

high

higher

highest

far

further

furthest

The Swing

How do you like to go up in a swing,
    Up in the air so blue?
Oh, I do think it the pleasantest thing
    Ever a child can do!

Up in the air and over the wall,
    Till I can see so wide,
Rivers and trees and cattle and all
    Over the countryside –

Till I look down on the garden green,
    Down on the roof so brown –
Up in the air I go flying again,
    Up in the air and down!

Robert Louis Stevenson

◣ SCHOLASTIC
PHOTOCOPIABLE

What forces are and what they do

A force is one thing
acting on another.

You can't see a force but you can often
see what it does.

What push and pull forces do is often
easy to see and identify because they
can get things moving.

Forces can make things move, stop,
speed up, slow down, change direction,
turn or change shape.

Because forces can't be seen they are
often talked about in terms of the effect
they have, like pushing, pulling, bending,
twisting, squeezing and stretching.

Push, pull or twist

▷ Find things at home that need a push, pull or twist to make them move or work.

These things have to be pushed

These things need to be pulled

These things have to be twisted

▷ Have you put some things in both the push and pull boxes, for example a drawer? List any others here.

USING ELECTRICITY

Content and skills

This chapter links to Unit 2F 'Using electricity' of the QCA Scheme of Work for science at Key Stage 1. The Using Electricity Resource Gallery on the CD-ROM, together with the teacher's notes and photocopiable pages in this chapter, can be used when teaching this unit. As with the QCA Scheme of Work, this chapter encourages children to think about the concept of electricity and the important role that it plays in our everyday lives.

The teacher's notes include ways of using the resources on the CD as a whole class, for group work or with individual children. Some of the activities suggested will link with other areas of the curriculum, such as English, maths, or design and technology. Wherever possible the activities encourage the children to ask questions and develop an enquiring approach to their learning.

Resources on the CD-ROM

There are photographs of electrical equipment that use mains electricity and with which the children may be familiar. Other photographs show equipment that use batteries as a source of energy, and some that can use either mains or batteries. There are diagrams of simple circuits that will help to ascertain whether or not the children have grasped the concept that a complete circuit is needed for a device to work.

Photocopiable pages

The photocopiable pages in the book are also provided in PDF format on the CD-ROM and can be printed out from there. They include:
▶ word cards containing the essential vocabulary of the topic
▶ a story
▶ a writing frame.

Science skills

Skills such as observing, questioning, describing, finding out, sorting, sequencing, listening, speaking, reading, writing and drawing are involved in the activities suggested in the teacher's notes in this chapter. For example, looking closely at drawings of simple circuits will help develop children's observation skills. Making simple circuits will help them to understand that a complete circuit is needed to make an electrical device work, and realise that there often needs to be a logical sequence of events before things will work.

Photographs © Ingram Publishing

NOTES ON THE CD-ROM RESOURCES

Diagrams of complete and incomplete circuits

Children need to understand that electrical devices will only work when there is a complete circuit, including an energy source. Any break in the circuit will cause a device not to work. For circuit work, 6v lantern batteries provide a stable, long lasting source . Never use rechargeable batteries for this sort of activity, since they can discharge very quickly if short circuited and become hot enough to cause a nasty burn. A single battery is more properly called a cell (usually 1.5v). A battery is composed of two or more cells, although they may be combined within a case so that the separate cells cannot be seen. Higher voltages may result in mild electric shocks. Avoid using the word *power* when talking about the energy source for electrical devices. Power has a specific scientific meaning not associated with electricity. It is better to use the correct scientific terminology, *energy*, from the start to avoid confusion later.

The children will need to have had lots of practical experience in making circuits before discussing the circuits provided here.

Discussing the diagrams
▶ Look at the diagrams and discuss them with the children. Can they name the various components in them?
▶ Which of the circuits do they think would work (A), and which would not (B, C, D, E, F, G and H)? Can they tell you why? (Because a complete circuit is needed to make it work.)
▶ Ask if any of the children can point out the break in the circuits.

Activities
▶ Give the children wires, batteries and bulbs and allow them to practise making and breaking simple circuits. Can they put a buzzer into the circuit instead of a bulb?
▶ Look at the word cards on photocopiable pages 75, 76 and 77 with the children and discuss the meaning of each word. Where appropriate, ask them to match the word to the component.
▶ Make several sets of the word cards on photocopiable pages 75, 76 and 77. Mount them on card and laminate them. Place all the cards face down on a table and let the children take it in turns to turn over a card until they have collected all the components to make a simple circuit. They should then arrange the cards in the correct order to make the circuit.
▶ Provide wires, bulbs and batteries for the children to make simple circuits.
▶ Ask the children to draw and label the circuits they have made, using the word cards on photocopiable pages 75 and 76 to help them. At this stage children are not required to use standard symbols, but some of them may like to design their own.

THINGS THAT USE MAINS ELECTRICITY

Toaster, Vacuum cleaner, Computer, Hair dryer

Electricity is so much a part of everyday life for most children that they probably don't realise the amount of equipment that relies on electricity as a source of energy. The photographs show equipment that most children will be familiar with. It is important that the children understand that electricity can be dangerous and all such equipment should be treated with care, however familiar they are with its use.

Discussing the photographs
▶ Look at the photographs with the children and ask them to name each object. Talk about what each of them does.
▶ Ask the children if they know what makes each object work. Talk about having to plug each machine into an electrical socket to connect it to the electricity supply.
▶ Talk about things the children have at home that use electricity. Encourage them to think about equipment they may find in each room and make lists of these on the board.
▶ Talk about the need for care when using electricity at home. Tell the children that electrical equipment should never be taken into a bathroom, or things other than a plug poked into an electrical socket. Stress the dangers of playing near pylons, sub-stations or railway lines.

Activities

▶ Take the children around the school to look for things that use mains electricity. Back in the classroom, ask the children to record what they found in words or pictures.

▶ Give the children a copy of the sheet 'Things at home that use electricity' (photocopiable page 80) and ask them to fill it in for homework, recording their findings in words or pictures.

▶ Give the children copies of the photographs, and any other photographs or pictures of objects that use mains electricity, and ask them to sort them according to what the object does. For example, things that make sound, provide heat or movement. Ask the children to explain the reasons for their groupings.

▶ Read the story 'The day the lines came down' (photocopiable page 78) to the class and ask the children to note all the things that stopped working when the electricity was cut off. What did the family do instead?

▶ Look at the photographs again and say what could be used or how the task could be carried out without that particular device. For example, hair could be rubbed dry with a towel.

THINGS THAT USE BATTERIES

Mobile phone, Torch, Car, Smoke alarm

Some of the devices in these photographs may use rechargeable batteries. These are quite safe if used properly and kept enclosed in their proper housing where there is no danger of a short circuit. It is often inconvenient to have a certain piece of electrical equipment connected to the mains supply as we want it to be more flexible and mobile, and this would be impossible without enormously long leads which would lead to all kinds of problems. Being able to store electricity in a battery enables us to use a device away from a mains supply.

Discussing the photographs

▶ Look at the photographs of the objects that use batteries. Ask the children to identify each object and talk about what they use to make them work. Each has a battery to supply the electricity it needs to work. Most of the batteries are quite small, but the car has a bigger, heavier, more powerful battery to provide the spark that ignites the petrol to make the engine turn over. A car with a flat battery will not start.

▶ Discuss why batteries are useful as energy sources. For example, it means that devices can be used away from a mains supply, making them mobile.

▶ Discuss the fact that batteries usually supply a much smaller voltage than the mains supply, making it safer for small equipment.

▶ Ask the children if any of them have toys that use batteries. Can they describe what they do and how they work? Can they find out what type of batteries they use?

Activities

▶ Ask the children to draw or design a picture of a toy that uses batteries.

▶ Show the children a selection of batteries. Are they all the same? How are they different? Focus on shape and voltage.

▶ Provide the children with a small selection of things that use batteries, but without the batteries fitted. Put the batteries on the table and ask the children to fit the correct battery into each device and make it work.

▶ Find out how long a battery lasts with the children. Plan an investigation to find out how long a battery will last. Use two torches to compare batteries of different makes, for instance.

THINGS THAT USE MAINS ELECTRICITY OR BATTERIES

Portable radio, Laptop computer

These photographs show two pieces of equipment that can use either batteries or a mains supply as an energy source. A radio or computer may be needed to work for extended periods and a battery would not be able to supply energy for that length of time. It is, therefore, convenient to be able to connect it to the mains supply, which can provide a constant supply and save the batteries for shorter periods of work.

Discussing the photographs

▶ Discuss why it is useful for objects to be able to use either mains electricity or batteries. Explain that battery operated objects are portable and convenient, but useless if the batteries are flat. It is useful then to be able to plug the device into the mains electricity supply.
▶ Talk about how some equipment uses rechargeable batteries, perhaps like their toothbrush. Ask, *How are these different from ordinary batteries?* (Rechargeable batteries can be re-energised from the mains using a special unit. Ordinary batteries need to be disposed of once all their energy has been used.) Remind the children never to try and take batteries apart.

Activities

▶ Make a list on the board of other things that can use either mains electricity or batteries. Which use rechargeable batteries?
▶ Let the children listen to a radio playing using batteries and then plugged into the mains supply. Ask the children, *Does it sound different? Do you have to adjust the volume? Will it still work connected to the mains supply but without any batteries in?*

NOTES ON THE PHOTOCOPIABLE PAGES

Word cards PAGE 75

These word cards contain some of the basic vocabulary for the children to use and learn when learning about 'Using electricity'. These include:
▶ words relating to circuits
▶ words relating to electricity.
Read through the words with the children and ask if there are any the children have heard before. Help them to look up any they don't understand and talk about their meaning.

Activities

▶ Give the children a selection of circuit components and ask them to match these to the appropriate words.
▶ Spread the word cards on the table and ask the children to find specific words.
▶ Use the word cards as a word bank to help the children label pictures or to help them with their writing.

The day the lines came down PAGE 78

This is a story to read to the children to encourage them to think about the effect that electricity has on our lives.

Discussing the story

▶ Talk about what it would be like if there was no electricity, particularly in the winter time.
▶ Ask the children to tell you some of the things that we rely on electricity to provide for us, such as hot water, heat and light.
▶ Ask the children if they had no electricity at home, what would they miss most?

Activities

▶ Read the story and ask the children to tell you all the things that did not work while the electricity was off. Make a list of these on the board.
▶ Talk about what Sally and her Mum did that was different from usual. Was there anything that Sally liked about having no electricity?
▶ Discuss what people did before electricity was discovered. For example, how did they boil the kettle or do the ironing?

Things at home that use electricity PAGE 80

This sheet could be done as a homework activity. The resulting lists may need to be treated sensitively if you have children from different backgrounds, in which case you might prefer the children to fill the sheet in at school. Read through the sheet and make sure the children understand what is needed. Talk about the things the children might look for at home.

Circuit word cards (1)

bulb

bulb holder

buzzer

battery

switch

component

Circuit word cards (2)

circuit

connection

mains

wire

break

complete

Electricity word cards

energy

light up

electricity

source

device

current

The day the lines came down

Sally woke up and immediately noticed something was different. There was usually a sort of hum about the house. She could often smell toast and the central heating made clicking noises in the pipes. There was also usually someone talking on the radio and when the mornings were dark, like today, she could see the glow of the light coming up from the kitchen.

This morning everything was very quiet. There was no smell of toast and when Sally poked her nose out of the bedclothes she noticed how cold it was – and how dark. She crawled out of bed and found her slippers and dressing gown. It was chilly. Perhaps it was still very early and Mum hadn't turned the heating up yet.

Sally went over and looked out of her bedroom window. She could see the trees bending in the wind and rain was bouncing off the workshop roof. The sky looked grey and dark clouds were scudding across it. She went downstairs to the kitchen. It was dark there too, and there was no steam coming out of the kettle and no friendly voice coming from the radio. Just then the back door opened and Mum came in. She was wrapped up in her thick coat and she had her wellies on.

"You're awake. I was leaving you in bed where it's warm," said Mum. "In the night the wind was so strong it blew that old tree in Mr Grimwood's garden down and it fell across the electricity wires and brought them down too, so we have no electricity. Your dad is down there now, helping to try to move the parts of the tree that are blocking the lane, but I'm afraid we shall have to wait for the electricity people to come and repair the wires."

"Let's get you dressed," said Mum, "before you get cold. You'll have to put on your warmest jumper because there's no heating. Without electricity the pump won't work to pump the water round the radiators, so the boiler won't come on."

Just then Dad came in with a pile of logs in his arms.

"We've managed to cut some of the branches off the tree and I've brought these to use on the fire in the living room. By the time you're dressed I'll have a fire going."

Sally went into the bathroom to have a wash and brush her teeth. When she turned on the tap there was no hot water, so she didn't linger too long. She hurriedly got dressed and went downstairs again. Dad had got the fire going and it was a little warmer in the living room at least.

"I'm sorry, but you'll have to have a drink of orange and some cornflakes for breakfast. The toaster needs electricity to work and so does the kettle," said Mum, "and we won't be able to cook a meal because the cooker is electric, too. I hope the electricity is not off for too long," continued Mum, "because I filled the freezer up yesterday. It will be OK for a few hours, but things will start to defrost if it's off too long."

Dad was searching in the kitchen drawer where they kept all sorts of odds and ends.

"Ah, there they are. I knew we had some somewhere."

He walked across the room holding four small batteries. He took the radio off the shelf and opened the back. He put the four batteries into the radio and turned it on. The friendly voice was there.

"Just in time for the news," said Dad.

According to the news they weren't the only people to have lost their electricity supply because of the storm. There were lots of trees blown down and the electricity engineers were out trying to reconnect everyone as fast as they could.

"If there are so many trees down they may not get round to us today," said Dad, "so we had better make sure that we have plenty of candles ready for tonight when it gets dark. We shall have to be very careful. We don't want to set the place on fire as well."

No one came to reconnect the electricity that day. Mum did manage to heat a pan of water on the fire in the front room, so they got a hot drink, but they had to have a sandwich for dinner instead of a hot meal. Mum said they would have to eat up some of the things in the fridge and freezer anyway and Sally was allowed as much ice cream as she wanted.

When it began to get dark, Mum lit the candles so that they could see. It really made the room very cosy, thought Sally, and she rather liked it.

"Can I watch my favourite programme please, Mum?" asked Sally.

"I'm sorry," said Mum, "but the TV won't work without electricity, but if you come and sit with me we can read a story together. We can just about see by the light of the candles."

So Sally curled up on the settee with Mum in front of the log fire, and together they read one of Sally's favourite stories. It was really rather cosy and Sally wasn't sure she wanted the people to come and mend the wires at all. But when it was time for bed, she realised how cold it was away from the fire. She stubbed her toe on the end of the bed because she couldn't see where she was going, and there was still no hot water in the tap!

Next morning it was still cold when Sally woke up.

"Good morning," said Mum, coming up the stairs. "The electricity repair people have come and it shouldn't be long before we are back to normal."

"Oh good," said Sally, "but Mum, could we sometimes curl up for a story in the dark, with candles, like we did last night?

Things at home that use electricity

In the living room I found

In my bedroom I found

In the kitchen I found

Other things I found: